Bienvenu!

# Just Enough
# FRENCH

# Just Enough
# FRENCH

## HOW TO GET BY AND
## BE EASILY UNDERSTOOD

### Second Edition

**McGraw·Hill**

New York   Chicago   San Francisco   Lisbon   London   Madrid   Mexico City
Milan   New Delhi   San Juan   Seoul   Singapore   Sydney   Toronto

The **McGraw·Hill** Companies

**Library of Congress Cataloging-in-Publication Data**

Ellis, D. L.
    Just enough French : how to get by and be easily understood /
D. L. Ellis, F. Clarke ; pronunciation, J. Baldwin.—2nd ed.
        p.   cm.
    Includes index.
    ISBN 0-07-145139-0

    1. French language—Conversation and phrase books—
English. I. Clarke, F. II. Title.

  PC2121.E45  2005
  448.3'421—dc22                                    2005047942

1 2 3 4 5 6 7 8 9 0   DOC/DOC   0 9 8 7 6 5

ISBN 0-07-145139-0

McGraw-Hill books are available at special quantity discounts
to use as premiums and sales promotions, or for use in corporate
training programs. For more information, please write to the Director
of Special Sales, Professional Publishing, McGraw-Hill, Two Penn
Plaza, New York, NY 10121-2298. Or contact your local bookstore.

This book is printed on acid-free paper.

# Contents

# Using This Phrase Book

This phrase book is designed to help you get by in France and countries where French is spoken, to get what you need or want. It concentrates on the simplest but most effective way that you can express your needs or desires in an unfamiliar language.

The Contents tells you which section of the book to consult for the phrase you need. The Index has a more detailed list of topics that are covered in this book.

When you have found the correct page, you are given either the exact phrase you need or help in making a suitable sentence. You will also be given help in pronunciation. Especially helpful are the sections that provide the likely responses French speakers may give to your questions.

To practice the basic nuts and bolts of the language further, we have included a "Do It Yourself" section at the end of the book.

The sections "Everyday Expressions," "Shop Talk," and "Public Notices" will be particularly useful, and you can expect to refer to them frequently.

Before you leave for France or Quebec, be sure to contact one of the tourist information offices listed below (see page14).

French Government Tourist Office
444 Madison Avenue
New York, NY 10022
(212) 838-7800

French Government Tourist Office
9454 Wilshire Boulevard, #715
Los Angeles, CA 90212
(310) 271-2358

French Government Tourist Office
676 N. Michigan Avenue, Suite 3360
Chicago, IL 60611
(312) 751-7800

Consulate General of France
31 Saint James Avenue, Suite 750
Boston, MA 02116
(617) 542-7374

Consulate General of France
3475 Piedmont Road NE, Suite 1840
Atlanta, GA 30305
(404) 495-1660

Quebec Government House
1 Rockefeller Plaza, 26th Floor
New York, NY 10020
(212) 843-0975

Canadian Government Office of Tourism
235 Queen Street, 4th Floor
Ottawa, ON  K1A 0H6
(613) 954-3850

# A Note on Pronunciation

In the typical French phrase book, there is a pronunciation key that tries to teach English-speaking tourists how to correctly pronounce French. This is based on the belief that in order to be understood, the tourist must pronounce every word almost like a native speaker would.

The authors of this book set out to devise a more workable and more usable pronunciation system. We considered the fact that it is impossible for an average speaker of English, with no training in phonetics and phonetic transcription, to reproduce the sounds of a foreign language perfectly. Further, we believe that you don't have to have perfect pronunciation in order to make yourself understood in a foreign language. After all, native speakers will take into account that you are visitors to their country; they will most likely feel gratified by your efforts to communicate and will go out of their way to try to understand you. We have also found that visitors to a foreign country are not usually concerned with perfect pronunciation—they just want to get their message across, to communicate!

With this in mind, we have designed a pronunciation system of the utmost simplicity. This system does not attempt to give a tedious, problematic representation of French sounds; instead, it uses common English sound and letter combinations that are closest to the sounds of French. Because in French it is important to say each syllable with equal emphasis, there is no indication for any individual syllable to carry more stress than any other syllable in a given word or phrase.

Practice makes perfect, so it is a good idea to repeat aloud to yourself the phrases you think you're going to use, before you actually use them. This will give you greater confidence and will help you to be understood.

You may want to pronounce French as well as possible, of course, and the present system is an excellent way to start. Since it uses only the sounds of English, however, you will very soon need to depart from it as you imitate the sounds you hear French speakers produce and begin to relate them to French spelling.

**Amusez-vous!** Have fun!

# Everyday Expressions

• See also "Shop Talk," p. 44.

| | |
|---|---|
| Hello./Good morning./<br>Good day./Good afternoon. | **Bonjour.**<br>bohn·shoor |
| Hello./Good morning./<br>Good day./Good afternoon. | **Salut.** (*friends only*)<br>sah·loo |
| Good evening. | **Bonsoir.**<br>bohn·swah |
| Good night. | **Bonne nuit.**<br>bun nwee |
| Good-bye. | **Au revoir.**<br>oh rev·wah |
| See you later. | **À tout à l'heure.**<br>ah too·tah·ler |
| Yes. | **Oui.**<br>wee |
| Please. | **S'il vous plaît.**<br>sil voo pleh |
| Yes, please. | **Oui, s'il vous plaît.**<br>wee sil voo pleh |
| Great! | **Formidable!**<br>for·mee·dahb |
| Thank you. | **Merci.**<br>mair·see |
| Thank you very much. | **Merci beaucoup.**<br>mair·see boh·coo |
| That's right. | **C'est exact.**<br>set ex·ah |
| No. | **Non.**<br>nohn |
| No, thank you. | **Non, merci.**<br>nohn mair·see |

(**Merci** by itself can also mean "No, thank you.")

| | |
|---|---|
| I disagree. | **Je ne suis pas d'accord.**<br>sher ner swee pah dah·cor |
| Excuse me./Sorry. | **Pardon.**<br>par·dohn |
| Don't mention it./That's okay. | **De rien.**<br>der ree·an |
| That's good./I like it. | **Ça va.**<br>sah vah |

| | |
|---|---|
| That's no good./I don't like it. | **Ça ne va pas.**<br>sah ner vah pah |
| I know. | **Je sais.**<br>sher seh |
| I don't know. | **Je ne sais pas.**<br>sher ner seh pah |
| It doesn't matter. | **Ça ne fait rien.**<br>sah ner feh ree·an |
| Where's the restroom, please? | **Où sont les WC, s'il vous plaît?**<br>oo sohn leh veh·seh sil voo pleh |
| How much is that? | **C'est combien, ça?**<br>seh com·bee·an sah |
| Is the tip included? | **Est-ce que le service est compris?**<br>es ker ler sair·veess eh com·pree |
| Do you speak English? | **Parlez-vous anglais?**<br>par·leh·voo·zahn·gleh |
| I'm sorry … | **Je regrette…**<br>sher rer·gret |
| … I don't speak French. | **je ne parle pas français.**<br>sher ner parl pah frahn·seh |
| … I only speak a little French. | **je parle très peu le français.**<br>sher parl treh per ler frahn·seh |
| … I don't understand. | **je ne comprends pas.**<br>sher ner com·prahn pah |
| Please, can you … | **S'il vous plaît, pouvez-vous…**<br>sil voo pleh poo·veh·voo |
| … repeat that? | **répéter?**<br>reh·peh·teh |
| … speak more slowly? | **parler plus lentement?**<br>par·leh ploo lahnt·mahn |
| … write it down? | **l'écrire?**<br>leh·creer |
| What is this called in French? | **Comment ça s'appelle en français?**<br>com·mahn sah sah·pel ahn<br>frahn·seh |

# Crossing the Border

## Essential Information

- Don't waste time before you leave rehearsing what you're going to say to the border officials—chances are, you won't have to say anything at all, especially if you travel by air.

- It is more useful to check that you have the following documents ready for the trip: passport, airline tickets, money, traveler's checks, insurance documents, driver's license, and car registration documents.

- Look for the following signs.

  **Douane**       Customs
  **Frontière**    Border

  For additional signs and notices, see p. 108.

- You may be asked routine questions by the customs officials, such as those below. If you have to provide personal information, see "Meeting People," p. 5. It is important to know how to say "nothing": **Rien** (ree·an).

## Routine Questions

| | |
|---|---|
| Passport? | **Passeport?**<br>pahss·por |
| Insurance? | **Assurance?**<br>ah·soo·rahns |
| Registration papers? | **Carte grise?**<br>cart greez |
| Ticket, please. | **Billet, s'il vous plaît.**<br>bee·yeh sil voo pleh |
| Do you have anything to declare? | **Avez-vous quelque chose à déclarer?**<br>ah·veh·voo kelker shohz ah deh·clah·reh |
| Where are you going? | **Où allez-vous?**<br>oo ah·leh·voo |
| How long are you staying? | **Combien de temps comptez-vous rester?**<br>com·bee·an der tahn con·teh·voo res·teh |
| Where are you coming from? | **D'où venez-vous?**<br>doo ver·neh voo |

You may also be required to fill out forms that ask for the following information.

| | |
|---|---|
| **nom** | last name |
| **prénom** | first name |
| **nom de jeune fille** | maiden name |
| **date de naissance** | date of birth |
| **lieu de naissance** | place of birth |
| **adresse** | address |
| **nationalité** | nationality |
| **profession** | profession |
| **numéro du passeport** | passport number |
| **fait à** | issued at |
| **signature** | signature |

# Meeting People

See also "Everyday Expressions," p. 1.

## Breaking the Ice

| | |
|---|---|
| Hello./Good morning./<br>Good day./Good afternoon. | **Bonjour.**<br>bohn·shoor |
| Hello./Good morning./<br>Good day./Good afternoon. | **Salut.** (*friends only*)<br>sah·loo |
| How are you? | **Ça va?**<br>sah vah |
| Pleased to meet you. | **Enchanté** (*male*)/<br>    **Enchantée** (*female*).<br>ahn·shahn·teh |
| I am here … | **Je suis ici…**<br>sher swee·zee·see |
| … on vacation. | **en vacances.**<br>ahn vah·cahns |
| … on business. | **pour affaires.**<br>poor ah·fair |
| Can I offer you … | **Puis-je vous offrir…**<br>pweesh voo·zoh·freer |
| … a drink? | **un verre?**<br>an vair |
| … a cigarette? | **une cigarette?**<br>oon see·gah·ret |
| … a cigar? | **un cigare?**<br>an see·gar |
| Are you staying long? | **Vous êtes ici pour longtemps?**<br>voo·zet ee·see poor long·tahn |

## Names

| | |
|---|---|
| What's your name? | **Comment vous appelez-vous?**<br>com·mahn voo·zah·pleh·voo |
| My name is _____. | **Je m'appelle _____.**<br>shmah·pel… |

# Family

| | |
|---|---|
| Are you married? | **Vous êtes marié** (*male*)/ **mariée** (*female*)**?** |
| | voo·zet mah·ree·eh |
| I am … | **Je suis…** |
| | sher swee |
| … married. | **marié** (*male*)/**mariée** (*female*)**.** |
| | mah·ree·eh |
| … single. | **célibataire.** |
| | seh·lee·bah·tair |
| This is … | **Voici…** |
| | vwah·see |
| … my wife. | **ma femme.** |
| | mah fam |
| … my husband. | **mon mari.** |
| | mohn mah·ree |
| … my son. | **mon fils.** |
| | mohn feess |
| … my daughter. | **ma fille.** |
| | mah fee |
| … my (boy)friend. | **mon ami.** |
| | moh·nah·mee |
| … my (girl)friend. | **mon amie.** |
| | moh·nah·mee |
| … my (male) colleague. | **mon collègue.** |
| | mohn coh·leg |
| … my (female) colleague. | **ma collègue.** |
| | mah coh·leg |
| Do you have any children? | **Avez-vous des enfants?** |
| | ah·veh·voo deh·zahn·fahn |
| I have … | **J'ai…** |
| | sheh |
| … one daughter. | **une fille.** |
| | oon fee |
| … one son. | **un fils.** |
| | an feess |
| … two daughters. | **deux filles.** |
| | der fee |
| … three sons. | **trois fils.** |
| | trwah feess |
| No, I don't have children. | **Non, je n'ai pas d'enfants.** |
| | nohn sher neh pah dahn·fahn |

## Where You Live

| Are you … | **Vous êtes…** |
| | voo·zet |
| … Belgian? | **belge?** |
| | belsh |
| … French? | **français** (*male*)/**française** (*female*)? |
| | frahn·seh/frahn·sez |
| … from Luxembourg? | **du Luxembourg?** |
| | doo look·sahn·boor |
| … Swiss? | **suisse?** |
| | sweess |
| I am American (*male*). | **Je suis américain** (*male*). |
| | sher swee·zah·meh·ree·can |
| I am American (*female*). | **Je suis américaine** (*female*). |
| | sher swee·zah·meh·ree·ken |

For other nationalities, see p. 122.

| I live … | **J'habite…** |
| | shah·beet |
| … in California. | **en Californie.** |
| | ahn cah·lee·for·nee |
| … in the United States. | **(les) États-Unis.** |
| | (lehz) eh·tah·zoo·nee |

For other countries, see p. 120.

| … in the north. | **dans le nord.** |
| | dahn ler nor |
| … in the south. | **dans le sud.** |
| | dahn ler sood |
| … in the east. | **dans l'est.** |
| | dahn lest |
| … in the west. | **dans l'ouest.** |
| | dahn loo·est |
| … downtown. | **dans le centre.** |
| | dahn ler sahnt |

## For the Businessman and Businesswoman

| I'm from _____ (*company's name*). | **Je travaille pour _____.** |
| | sher trah·vye poor… |
| I have an appointment with _____. | **J'ai rendez-vous avec _____.** |
| | sheh rahn·deh·voo·zah·vek… |

May I speak to _____?

**Puis-je parler à _____?**
pweesh par·leh ah…

Here is my card.

**Voici ma carte.**
vwah·see mah cart

I'm sorry I'm late.

**Je m'excuse d'être en retard.**
sher mex·cooz det·rahn rer·tar

Can I make another appointment?

**Puis-je prendre un autre rendez-vous?**
pweesh prahn·dran oh·trahn·deh·voo

I'm staying at the (Paris) Hotel.

**Je suis à l'hôtel (Paris).**
sher swee·zah loh·tel (pah·ree)

I'm staying on (St. John's) Road.

**Je suis dans la rue (St. Jean).**
sher swee dahn lah roo (san shahn)

# Asking Directions

## Essential Information

- You will find the names of the following places on shops, maps, and public signs and notices.

## What to Say

| | |
|---|---|
| Excuse me, please. | **Pardonnez-moi, s'il vous plaît.**<br>par·doh·neh·mwah sil voo pleh |
| How do I get … | **Pour aller…**<br>Poor ah·leh |
| … to Paris? | **à Paris?**<br>ah pah·ree |
| … to St. Pierre Street? | **à la rue Saint-Pierre?**<br>ah lah roo san·pyair |
| … to the Hotel Metropole? | **à l'hôtel Métropole?**<br>ah loh·tel meh·troh·pohl |
| … to the airport? | **à l'aéroport?**<br>ah lah·air·roh·por |
| … to the beach? | **à la plage?**<br>ah lah plash |
| … to the bus station? | **à la gare d'autobus?**<br>ah lah gar doh·toh·boos |
| … to downtown? | **au centre de la ville?**<br>oh sahnt der lah veel |
| … to the historic site? | **au site historique?**<br>oh seet ee·stoh·reek |
| … to the market? | **au marché?**<br>oh mar·sheh |
| … to the police station? | **au commissariat?**<br>oh com·mees·sah·ree·ah |
| … to the port? | **au port?**<br>oh por |
| … to the post office? | **à la poste?**<br>ah lah post |
| … to the train station? | **à la gare?**<br>ah lah gar |
| … to the sports stadium? | **au stade?**<br>oh stahd |
| … to the tourist information office? | **au syndicate d'initiative?**<br>oh san·dee·cah dee·nee·see·ah·teev |
| … to the town hall? | **à la mairie?**<br>ah lah mair·ee |

| | |
|---|---|
| Excuse me, please. | **Pardonnez-moi, s'il vous plaît.**<br>par·doh·neh·mwah sil voo pleh |
| Is there ... nearby? | **Est-ce qu'il y a... près d'ici?**<br>es keel yah... preh dee·see |
| ... an art gallery ... | **un musée d'art**<br>an moo·zeh dar |
| ... a bakery ... | **une boulangerie**<br>oon boo·lahn·shree |
| ... a bank ... | **une banque**<br>oon bahnk |
| ... a bar ... | **un bar**<br>an bar |
| ... a botanical garden ... | **un jardin botanique**<br>an shar·dan boh·tah·neek |
| ... a bus stop ... | **un arrêt d'autobus**<br>an ah·reh doh·toh·boos |
| ... a butcher ... | **une boucherie**<br>oon boo·shree |
| ... a café ... | **un café**<br>an cah·feh |
| ... a campsite ... | **un camping**<br>an cahm·ping |
| ... a candy store ... | **une confiserie**<br>oon cohn·fee·sree |
| ... a church ... | **une église**<br>oon eh·gleez |
| ... a cinema ... | **un cinéma**<br>an see·neh·mah |
| ... a currency exchange ... | **un bureau de change**<br>an byoo·roh der shahnsh |
| ... a delicatessen ... | **une charcuterie**<br>oon shar·coo·tree |
| ... a dentist's office ... | **un dentiste**<br>an dahn·teest |
| ... a department store ... | **un grand magasin**<br>an grahn mah·gah·zan |
| ... a disco ... | **une discothèque**<br>oon dees·coh·tek |
| ... a doctor's office ... | **un docteur**<br>an doc·ter |
| ... a drugstore ... | **une pharmacie**<br>oon far·mah·see |
| ... a dry cleaner's ... | **un pressing**<br>an press·ing |

| | |
|---|---|
| Is there … nearby? | **Est-ce qu'il y a… près d'ici?** |
| | es keel yah… preh dee·see |
| … a fish market … | **une poissonnerie** |
| | oon pwah·sohn·ree |
| … a garage (*for repairs*) … | **un garage** |
| | an gah·rahsh |
| … a gas station … | **une station service** |
| | oon stah·syohn sair·veess |
| … a grocery … | **une épicerie** |
| | oon eh·pee·sree |
| … a hairdresser's … | **un coiffeur** |
| | an kwah·fer |
| … a hardware store … | **une quincaillerie** |
| | oon kan·kay·ree |
| … a hospital … | **un hôpital** |
| | an oh·pee·tahl |
| … a hotel … | **un hôtel** |
| | an oh·tel |
| … an ice-cream parlor … | **un glacier** |
| | an glah·see·eh |
| … a laundromat … | **une laverie** |
| | oon lahv·ree |
| … a mailbox … | **une boîte à lettres** |
| | oon bwaht ah let |
| … a museum … | **un musée** |
| | an moo·zeh |
| … a newsstand … | **un marchand de journaux** |
| | an mar·shahn der shoor·noh |
| … a nightclub … | **une boîte de nuit** |
| | oon bwaht der nwee |
| … a park (public garden) … | **un jardin public** |
| | an shar·dan poo·bleek |
| … a parking lot … | **un parking** |
| | an par·king |
| … a pastry shop … | **une pâtisserie** |
| | oon pah·teess·ree |
| … a pharmacy … | **une pharmacie** |
| | oon far·mah·see |
| … a public restroom … | **des WC publics** |
| | deh veh·seh poo·bleek |
| … a restaurant … | **un restaurant** |
| | an reh·stoh·rahn |
| … a (snack) bar … | **un snack** |
| | an snak |

| | |
|---|---|
| Excuse me, please. | **Pardonnez-moi, s'il vous plaît.**<br>par·doh·neh·mwah sil voo pleh |
| Is there … nearby? | **Est-ce qu'il y a… près d'ici?**<br>es keel yah… preh dee·see |
| … a Social Security Office … | **un bureau de la Sécurité Sociale**<br>an byoo·roh der lah seh·coo·ree·teh<br>soh·see·ahl |
| … a sports field … | **un terrain de sport**<br>an teh·ran der spor |
| … a streetcar stop … | **un arrêt de tram**<br>an ah-reh der tram |
| … a subway station … | **une station de métro**<br>oon stah-syohn der meh-troh |
| … a supermarket … | **un supermarché**<br>an soo·pair·mar·sheh |
| … a swimming pool … | **une piscine**<br>oon pee·seen |
| … a taxi stand … | **une station de taxis**<br>oon stah·syohn der tahx·ee |
| … a telephone … | **un téléphone**<br>an teh·leh·fohn |
| … a theater … | **un théâtre**<br>an teh·aht |
| … a tobacco shop … | **un bureau de tabac**<br>an byoo·roh der tah·bah |
| … a travel agency … | **une agence de voyage**<br>oon ah·shahns der vwah·yahsh |
| … a vegetable market … | **un marchand de légumes**<br>an mar·shahn der leh·goom |
| … a youth hostel … | **une auberge de jeunesse**<br>oon oh·bairsh der sher·ness |
| … a zoo … | **un zoo**<br>an zoh·oh |

## Directions

- Asking where a place is, or if a place is nearby, is one thing; making sense of the answer is another. Here are some of the most common directions and replies you will receive.

| | |
|---|---|
| left | **gauche**<br>gohsh |
| right | **droite**<br>drwaht |

| | |
|---|---|
| straight ahead | **tout droit**<br>too drwah |
| there | **là**<br>lah |
| first left/right | **la première rue à gauche/droite**<br>lah preh·myair roo ah gohsh/<br>drwaht |
| second left/right | **la deuxième rue à gauche/droite**<br>lah der·zee·em roo ah gohsh/<br>drwaht |
| at the crossroad | **au carrefour**<br>oh car·foor |
| at the intersection | **à l'intersection**<br>ah lan·tair·sek·syohn |
| at the traffic light | **aux feux**<br>oh fer |
| at the traffic circle | **au rond-point**<br>oh rohn·pwen |
| at the grade crossing | **au passage à niveau**<br>oh pah·sahsh ah nee·voh |
| It's near/far. | **C'est près/loin.**<br>seh preh/lwen |
| one kilometer | **un kilomètre**<br>an kee·loh·met |
| two kilometers | **deux kilomètres**<br>der kee·loh·met |
| Five minutes … | **Cinq minutes…**<br>sank mee·noot |
| … on foot. | **à pied.**<br>ah pee·eh |
| … by car. | **en voiture.**<br>ahn vwah·toor |
| Take … | **Prenez…**<br>prer·neh |
| … the bus. | **l'autobus.**<br>loh·toh·boos |
| … the streetcar. | **le tram.**<br>ler tram |
| … the subway. | **le métro.**<br>ler meh·troh |
| … the train. | **le train.**<br>ler tran |

For public transportation, see p. 99.

# The Tourist Information Office

## Essential Information

- Most towns and many villages in France have a tourist information office. Look for the following signs.

  **Syndicat d'Initiative**
  **Office de Tourisme**
  **Fédération Nationale des Offices de Tourisme et Syndicats d'Initiative**

- Sometimes there are signs with the following abbreviations: **SI**, **OT**, or **FNOT-SI**.

- Information is also available from offices of the Automobile Club (**Automobile Club de France**), which uses the abbreviation **ACF**.

- For finding a tourist information office, see p. 9.

## What to Say

| | |
|---|---|
| Please, do you have … | **S'il vous plaît, avez-vous…**<br>sil voo pleh ah·veh·voo |
| … a map of the town? | **un plan de la ville?**<br>an plahn der lah veel |
| … a list of bus tours? | **une liste d'excursions en car?**<br>oon leest dex·coor·syohn an car |
| … a list of campsites? | **une liste de campings?**<br>oon leest der cahm·ping |
| … a list of events? | **une liste d'événements?**<br>oon leest deh·veh·ner·mahn |
| … a list of hotels? | **une liste d'hôtels?**<br>oon leest doh·tel |
| … a list of restaurants? | **une liste de restaurants?**<br>oon leest der reh·stoh·rahn |
| … a brochure on the town? | **une brochure sur la ville?**<br>oon broh·shoor soor lah veel |
| … a brochure on the region? | **une brochure sur la région?**<br>oon broh·shoor soor lah reh·shyohn |
| … a bus schedule? | **un horaire des autobus?**<br>an oh·rair deh·zoh·toh·boos |
| … a train schedule? | **un horaire des trains?**<br>an oh·rair deh tran |
| In English, please. | **En anglais, s'il vous plaît.**<br>ahn ahn·gleh sil voo pleh |

How much do I owe you?

**Combien vous dois-je?**
com·bee·an voo dwahsh

Can you recommend …

**Pouvez-vous recommander…**
poo·veh·voo rer·com·mahn·deh

… an inexpensive hotel?

**un hôtel bon marché?**
an oh·tel bohn mar·sheh

… an inexpensive restaurant?

**un restaurant bon marché?**
an reh·stoh·rahn bohn mar·sheh

Can you make a reservation
for me?

**Pouvez-vous me faire une
réservation?**
poo·veh·voo mer fair oon
reh·zair·vah·syohn

## Likely Answers

- When the answer is "no," you should be able to tell by the person's facial expression, tone of voice, or gesture, but there are language clues, such as the following.

No.

**Non.**
nohn

I'm sorry.

**Je regrette.**
sher rer·gret

I don't have a list of campsites.

**Je n'ai pas la liste des campings.**
sher neh pah lah leest deh
cahm·ping

I don't have any more left.

**Il ne m'en reste plus.**
il ner mahn rest ploo

It's free.

**C'est gratuit.**
seh grah·twee

# Accommodations

## Hotel

### Essential Information

- If you want hotel-type accommodations, look for the following signs.

  **Hôtel**
  **Motel**
  **Pension**  A small, privately run hotel
  **Auberge**  An often picturesque hotel in the countryside

- Lists of hotels and **pensions** can be obtained from local tourist offices of the Canadian Government Office of Tourism in Ottawa or the French Government Tourist Office in New York and other major cities (see p. ix).

- Since the price is displayed in the room itself, you can check it as you are looking at the room before agreeing to stay. The displayed price is for the room itself—per night, not per person. Breakfast is extra and therefore optional.

- Other than breakfast, not all hotels provide meals. A **pension** always provides meals. Breakfast is continental style: coffee or tea, rolls and/or croissants, and butter and jam.

- Some form of identification, like a passport or driver's license, is requested when you register at a hotel; the ID is normally kept overnight.

- Look for the words **service compris/non compris** (tip included/not included) on your bill in order to know whether you should tip an additional amount. It is normal practice, however, to tip porters.

- To ask directions to a hotel, see p. 9.

### What to Say

| | |
|---|---|
| I have a reservation. | **J'ai une réservation.**<br>sheh oon reh·zair·vah·syohn |
| Do you have any vacancies, please? | **Avez-vous des chambres libres, s'il vous plaît?**<br>ah·veh·voo deh shahmb leeb<br>sil voo pleh |
| Can I reserve a room? | **Puis-je réserver une chambre?**<br>pweesh reh·zair·veh oon shahmb |

It's for …

C'est pour…
seh poor

… one person.

une personne.
oon pair·son

… two people.

deux personnes.
der pair·son

For numbers, see p. 112.

For numbers, see p. 112.

It's for …

C'est pour…
seh poor

… one night.

une nuit.
oon nwee

… two nights.

deux nuits.
der nwee

… one week.

une semaine.
oon ser·men

… two weeks.

deux semaines.
der ser·men

I would like …

Je voudrais…
sher voo·dreh

… a room …

une chambre
oon shahmb

… two rooms …

deux chambres
der shahmb

… with a single bed.

à un lit.
ah an lee

… with two single beds.

à deux lits.
ah der lee

… with a double bed.

avec un grand lit.
ah·vek an grahn lee

… with a toilet.

avec WC.
ah·vek veh·seh

… with a bathroom.

avec salle de bains.
ah·vek sahl der ban

… with a shower.

avec douche.
ah·vek doosh

… with a cot.

avec un lit d'enfant.
ah·vek an lee dahn·fahn

… with a balcony.

avec balcon.
ah·vek bahl·cohn

I would like …

Je voudrais…
sher voo·dreh

… full board.

pension complète.
pahn·syohn com·plet

I would like …

**Je voudrais…**
sher voo·dreh

… half board.

**demi-pension.**
der·mee pahn·syohn

… bed and breakfast.

**chambre et petit déjeuner.**
shahmb eh ptee deh·shneh

Do you serve meals?

**Est-ce que vous faites restaurant?**
Es ker voo fet reh·stoh·rahn

At what time is …

**À quelle heure est…**
ah kel er eh

… breakfast?

**le petit déjeuner?**
ler ptee deh·shneh

… lunch?

**le déjeuner?**
ler deh·shneh

… dinner?

**le dîner?**
ler dee·neh

How much is it?

**C'est combien?**
seh com·bee·an

Can I look at the room?

**Puis-je voir la chambre?**
Pweesh vvah lah shahmb

I'd prefer a room …

**J'aimerais mieux une chambre…**
sheh·mreh mee·er oon shahmb

… in the front/in the back.

**sur le devant/sur le derrière.**
soor ler der·vahn/soor ler deh·ryair

I would like a quiet room.

**Je voudrais une chambre
tranquille.**
sher voo·dreh oon shahmb
trahn·keel

Okay, I'll take it.

**D'accord, je la prends.**
dah·cor sher lah prahn

No, thanks, I won't take it.

**Non, merci, je ne la prends pas.**
nohn mair·see sher ner lah prahn
pah

The key to number (10), please.

**La clé du (dix), s'il vous plaît.**
lah cleh doo (deess) sil voo pleh

Please, may I have …

**S'il vous plaît, puis-je avoir…**
sil voo pleh pweesh ah·vwah

… an ashtray?

**un cendrier?**
an sahn·dree·eh

… another blanket?

**une autre couverture?**
oon oht coo·vair·toor

… a coat hanger?

**un cintre?**
an sant

| | |
|---|---|
| Please, may I have … | **S'il vous plaît, puis-je avoir…**<br>sil voo pleh pweesh ah·vwah |
| … a glass? | **un verre?**<br>an vair |
| … another pillow? | **un autre oreiller?**<br>an oh·troh·reh·yeh |
| … some soap? | **du savon?**<br>doo sah·vohn |
| … a towel? | **une serviette?**<br>oon sair·vyet |
| Come in! | **Entrez!**<br>ahn·treh |
| One moment, please! | **Un moment, s'il vous plaît!**<br>an moh·mahn sil voo pleh |
| Please can you … | **S'il vous plaît, pouvez-vous…**<br>sil voo pleh poo·veh·voo |
| … do this laundry/dry cleaning? | **laver ceci/nettoyer ceci?**<br>lah·veh ser·see/net·wah·yeh ser·see |
| … call me at (seven o'clock)? | **m'appeler à (sept heures)?**<br>mah·pleh ah (set er) |
| … help me with my luggage? | **m'aider à porter mes bagages?**<br>meh·deh ah por·teh meh bah·gahsh |
| … call me a taxi for (nine o'clock)? | **m'appeler un taxi pour (neuf heures)?**<br>mah·pleh an tahx·ee poor (nerf er) |

For telling time, see p. 114.

| | |
|---|---|
| The bill, please. | **La note, s'il vous plaît.**<br>lah noht sil voo pleh |
| Is the tip included? | **Est-ce que le service est compris?**<br>es ker ler sair·veess eh com·pree |
| I think this is wrong. | **Je crois qu'il y a une erreur.**<br>sher crwah keel ya oon air·er |
| May I have a receipt? | **Puis-je avoir un reçu?**<br>pweesh ah·vwah an rer·soo |

## AT BREAKFAST

| | |
|---|---|
| Some more …, please. | **Encore…, s'il vous plaît.**<br>ahn·cor… sil voo pleh |
| … coffee … | **du café**<br>doo cah·feh |

| | |
|---|---|
| Some more …, please. | **Encore…, s'il vous plaît.**<br>ahn·cor… sil voo pleh |
| … tea … | **du thé**<br>doo teh |
| … bread … | **du pain**<br>doo pan |
| … butter … | **du beurre**<br>doo ber |
| … jam … | **de la confiture**<br>der lah cohn·fee·toor |
| May I have a boiled egg? | **Puis-je avoir un œuf à la coque?**<br>pweesh ah·vwah an erf ah lah cohk |

## Likely Reactions

| | |
|---|---|
| Do you have some identification, please? | **Avez-vous une pièce d'identité, s'il vous plaît?**<br>ah·veh·voo oon pee·ess dee·dahn·tee·teh sil voo pleh |
| What's your name? | **Quel est votre nom?**<br>kel eh voht nohm |
| Sorry, we're full. | **Je regrette, c'est complet.**<br>sher rer·gret seh com·pleh |
| I don't have any rooms left. | **Je n'ai plus de chambres.**<br>sher neh ploo der shahmb |
| Do you want to have a look? | **Vous voulez voir?**<br>voo voo·leh vwah |
| How many people is it for? | **C'est pour combien de personnes?**<br>seh poor com·bee·an der pair·son |
| From (seven o'clock) onwards. | **À partir de (sept heures).**<br>ah par·teer der (set er) |
| From (midday) onwards. | **À partir de (midi).**<br>ah par·teer der (mee·dee) |

For telling time, see p. 114.

| | |
|---|---|
| It's (15) euros. | **C'est (quinze) euros.**<br>seh (kanz) er·oh |

For numbers, see p. 112.

# Camping and Youth Hosteling

## Essential Information

### CAMPING

- Look for the word **Camping** or the sign below.

- Be prepared to have to pay:

  per person
  for the car (if applicable)
  for the tent or trailer space
  for electricity
  for a hot shower

- You must provide proof of identity, such as your passport.
- You can obtain lists of campsites from local tourist offices (see p. 14) or from the government tourist offices (see p. ix).
- Some campsites offer discounts to campers with the International Camping Carnet and some offer weekly or monthly rates.
- Officially recognized campsites have a star rating (like hotels).
- Municipality-run campsites are often reasonably priced and well run.
- Off-site camping (**le camping sauvage**) is prohibited in many areas. As a rule it is better and safer to use recognized sites.

### YOUTH HOSTELS

- Look for the words **Auberge de jeunesse**.
- You will be asked for your Youth Hostels Association (YHA) card and your passport upon arrival.
- Food and cooking facilities vary from hostel to hostel, and you may have to help with domestic chores.

- You must take your own sleeping bag lining, but bedding can sometimes be rented upon arrival.

- In peak season it is advisable to book beds in advance; your stay will be limited to a maximum of three consecutive nights per hostel.

- Apply to the government tourist offices (see p. ix) or to the local tourist offices in France (see p. 14) for lists of youth hostels and details of hostel regulations.

- For buying or replacing camping equipment, see p. 42.

## What to Say

| | |
|---|---|
| I have a reservation. | **J'ai une réservation.**<br>sheh oon reh·zair·vah·syohn |
| Do you have any vacancies? | **Avez-vous de la place?**<br>ah·veh·voo der lah plahss |
| It's for … | **C'est pour…**<br>seh poor |
| … one adult/one person … | **un adulte/une personne**<br>an ah·doolt/oon pair·son |
| … two adults/two people … | **deux adultes/deux personnes**<br>der·zah·doolt/der pair·son |
| … and one child. | **et un enfant.**<br>eh an ahn·fahn |
| … and two children. | **et deux enfants.**<br>eh der·zahn·fahn |
| It's for … | **C'est pour…**<br>seh poor |
| … one night. | **une nuit.**<br>oon nwee |
| … two nights. | **deux nuits.**<br>der nwee |
| … one week. | **une semaine.**<br>oon ser·men |
| … two weeks. | **deux semaines.**<br>der ser·men |
| How much is it … | **C'est combien…**<br>seh com·bee·an |
| … for the tent? | **pour la tente?**<br>poor lah tahnt |
| … for the trailer? | **pour la caravane?**<br>poor lah cah·rah·vahn |
| … for the car? | **pour la voiture?**<br>poor lah vwah·toor |

| | |
|---|---|
| How much is it … | **C'est combien…**<br>seh com·bee·an |
| … for the electricity? | **pour l'électricité?**<br>poor leh·lek·tree·see·teh |
| … per person? | **par personne?**<br>par pair·son |
| … per day/night? | **par jour/nuit?**<br>par shoor/nwee |
| May I look around? | **Puis-je voir?**<br>pweesh vwah |
| Do you close the gate at night? | **Est-ce que vous fermez le portail la nuit?**<br>es ker voo fair·meh ler por·tye lah nwee |
| Do you provide anything … | **Est-ce qu'on peut avoir…**<br>es kohn per ah·vwah |
| … to eat? | **de la nourriture?**<br>der lah noo·ree·toor |
| … to drink? | **des boissons?**<br>deh bwah·sohn |
| Is there/Are there … | **Est-ce qu'il y a…**<br>es keel yah |
| … a bar? | **un bar?**<br>an bar |
| … hot showers? | **des douches chaudes?**<br>deh doosh shohd |
| … a kitchen? | **une cuisine?**<br>oon kwee·zeen |
| … a laundry room? | **une laverie?**<br>oon lahv·ree |
| … a restaurant? | **un restaurant?**<br>an reh·stoh·rahn |
| … a shop? | **un magasin?**<br>an mah·gah·zan |
| … a swimming pool? | **une piscine?**<br>oon pee·seen |
| … a carry-out restaurant? | **des plats à emporter?**<br>deh plah ah ahm·por·teh |

For food shopping, see p. 48.

For eating and drinking out, see p. 67.

| | |
|---|---|
| I would like a pass for the shower. | **Je voudrais un jeton pour la douche.**<br>sher voo·dreh an sher·tohn poor lah doosh |
| Where are … | **Où sont…**<br>oo sohn |
| … the garbage cans? | **les poubelles?**<br>leh poo·bel |
| … the showers? | **les douches?**<br>leh doosh |
| … the toilets? | **les WC?**<br>leh veh·seh |
| At what time must one … | **À quelle heure doit-on…**<br>ah kel er dwah·tohn |
| … go to bed? | **se coucher?**<br>ser coo·sheh |
| … get up? | **se lever?**<br>ser ler·veh |
| Please, do you have … | **S'il vous plaît, avez-vous…**<br>sil voo pleh ah·veh·voo |
| … a broom? | **un balai?**<br>an bah·lye |
| … a can opener? | **un ouvre-boîte?**<br>an oov·bwaht |
| … a corkscrew? | **un tire-bouchon?**<br>an teer·boo·shohn |
| … any detergent (powder)? | **de la lessive?**<br>der lah leh·seev |
| … any detergent (liquid)? | **du liquide pour la vaisselle?**<br>doo lee·keed poor lah veh·sel |
| … a dish towel? | **un torchon?**<br>an tor·shohn |
| … a fork? | **une fourchette?**<br>oon foor·shet |
| … a frying pan? | **une poêle?**<br>oon pwahl |
| … an iron? | **un fer à repasser?**<br>an fair ah rer·pah·seh |
| … a knife? | **un couteau?**<br>an coo·toh |
| … a plate? | **une assiette?**<br>oon ah·syet |
| … a refrigerator? | **un frigo?**<br>an free·goh |

Please, do you have … **S'il vous plaît, avez-vous…**
sil voo pleh ah·veh·voo

… a saucepan? **une casserole?**
oon cahs·rohl

… a teaspoon? **une cuillère à café?**
oon kwee·yair ah cah·feh

The bill, please. **La note, s'il vous plaît.**
lah noht sil voo pleh

## PROBLEMS

The electric socket … **La prise de courant…**
lah preez der coo·rahn

The faucet … **Le robinet…**
ler roh·bee·neh

The light … **La lumière…**
lah loo·myair

The shower … **La douche…**
lah doosh

The toilet … **Le WC…**
ler veh·seh

… is not working. **ne marche pas.**
ner marsh pah

My camping gas has run out. **Je n'ai plus de gaz.**
sher neh ploo der gahz

## Likely Reactions

Do you have any **Avez-vous une pièce d'identité?**
identification? ah·veh·voo oon pee·ess
dee·dahn·tee·teh

Your membership card, please. **Votre carte, s'il vous plaît.**
voht cart sil voo pleh

What's your name, please? **Votre nom, s'il vous plaît.**
voht nohm sil voo pleh

Sorry, we're full. **Je regrette, c'est complet.**
sher rer·gret seh com·pleh

How many people is it for? **C'est pour combien de personnes?**
seh poor com·bee·an der pair·son

How many nights is it for? **C'est pour combien de nuits?**
seh poor com·bee·an der nwee

It's (5) euros … **C'est (cinq) euros…**
seh (sank) er·oh

… per day. **par jour.**
par shoor

It's (5) euros …

**C'est (cinq) euros…**
seh (sank) er·oh

… per night.

**par nuit.**
par nwee

For numbers, see p. 112.

# Rented Lodging

## Essential Information

- If you're looking for lodging to rent, look for the following words in advertising and on signs.

| | |
|---|---|
| **À louer** | For rent |
| **Appartement** | Apartment |
| **Chalet** | Cottage |
| **Ferme** | Farmhouse |
| **Maison** | House |
| **Studio** | Small apartment, studio |
| **Villa** | Detached house with garden |

- For arranging details of your rental, see "Hotel," p. 16.

- If you rent on the spot, you will need to know the following words.

| | |
|---|---|
| deposit | **les arrhes**<br>leh·zar |
| key | **la clé**<br>lah cleh |

- Having arranged your accommodation and arrived with the key, check the basic amenities that you take for granted at home.

- *Electricity:* Voltage? You may need an adapter for razors and small appliances brought from home.

- *Gas:* Municipal (natural) gas or bottled gas? Butane gas must be kept indoors, and propane gas must be kept outdoors.

- *Stove:* Don't be surprised to find the grill inside the oven (or no grill at all); a lid covering the burners that lifts up to form a backsplash; or a combination of two gas burners and two electric burners.

- *Toilet:* Sewer drainage or septic tank? Don't flush disposable diapers or similar materials down the toilet if you have a septic tank.

- *Water:* Locate the shut-off valve. Check faucets and plugs—they may not operate the way you are used to. Be sure you know how to turn on (or light) the hot water heater.
- *Windows:* Learn how to open and close windows and shutters.
- *Insects:* Is an insecticide provided? If not, buy one.
- *Equipment:* See p. 42 for buying or replacing equipment.
- You will probably deal with a real estate agent, but find out whom to contact in an emergency; it may be a neighbor who is renting the lodging to you.

## What to Say

| | |
|---|---|
| My name is _____ . | **Je m'appelle _____ .** <br> shmah·pel… |
| I'm staying at _____ . | **Je suis à _____ .** <br> sher swee-zah… |
| They have cut off … | **On a coupé…** <br> ohn ah coo·peh |
| … the electricity. | **l'électricité.** <br> leh·lek·tree·see·teh |
| … the gas. | **le gaz.** <br> ler gahz |
| … the water. | **l'eau.** <br> loh |
| Is there … in the area? | **Est-ce qu'il y a… par ici?** <br> es keel yah… par ee·see |
| … an electrician … | **un électricien** <br> an eh·lek·tree·see·an |
| … a plumber … | **un plombier** <br> an plohm·byeh |
| … a gas man … | **un employé du gaz** <br> an ahm·plwah·yeh doo gahz |
| Where is … | **Où est…** <br> oo eh |
| … the furnace/boiler? | **la chaudière?** <br> lah shoh·dyair |
| … the fuse box? | **la boîte à fusibles?** <br> lah bwaht ah foo·zeeb |
| … the water heater? | **le chauffe-eau?** <br> ler shohf·oh |
| … the water line shut-off valve? | **le robinet d'arrêt?** <br> ler roh·bee·neh dah·reh |

Is there …  
**Est-ce qu'il y a…**  
es keel yah

… municipal gas?  
**le gaz de ville?**  
ler gahz der veel

… bottled gas?  
**du gaz en bouteille?**  
doo gahz ahn boo·tay

… a septic tank?  
**une fosse septique?**  
oon foss sep·teek

… central heating?  
**le chauffage central?**  
ler shoh·fahsh sahn·trahl

The hair dryer …  
**Le séchoir à cheveux…**  
ler seh·shwah ah sher·ver

The heating system …  
**Le chauffage…**  
ler shoh·fahsh

The immersion heater …  
**Le chauffe-bains…**  
ler shohf·ban

The iron …  
**Le fer à repasser…**  
ler fair ah rer·pah·seh

The pilot light …  
**La veilleuse…**  
lah veh·yerz

The refrigerator …  
**Le réfrigérateur…**  
ler reh·free·sheh·rah·ter

The stove …  
**La cuisinière…**  
lah kwee·zee·nyair

The telephone …  
**Le téléphone…**  
ler teh·leh·fohn

The toilet …  
**Le WC…**  
ler veh·seh

The washing machine …  
**La machine à laver…**  
lah mah·sheen ah lah·veh

… is not working.  
**ne marche pas.**  
ner marsh pah

Where can I get …  
**Où puis-je trouver…**  
oo pweesh troo·veh

… an adapter for this?  
**un adaptateur pour ceci?**  
an ah·dahp·tah·ter poor ser·see

… a fuse?  
**un fusible?**  
an foo·zeeb

… insecticide?  
**une bombe insecticide?**  
oon bomb an·sek·tee·seed

… a light bulb?  
**une ampoule électrique?**  
oon ahm·pool eh·lek·treek

… a tank of butane gas?  
**une bouteille de gaz butane?**  
oon boo·tay der gahz boo·tahn

| | |
|---|---|
| Where can I get … | **Où puis-je trouver…**<br>oo pweesh troo·veh |
| … a tank of propane gas? | **une bouteille de gaz propane?**<br>oon boo·tay der gahz proh·pahn |
| The drain … | **Le tuyau…**<br>ler twee·yoh |
| The sink … | **L'évier…**<br>lehv·yeh |
| The toilet … | **Le WC…**<br>ler veh·seh |
| … is blocked. | **est bouché.**<br>eh boo·sheh |
| The gas is leaking. | **Il y a une fuite de gaz.**<br>il yah oon fweet der gahz |
| Can you repair it right away? | **Pouvez-vous le réparer tout<br>de suite?**<br>poo·veh·voo ler reh·pah·reh toot<br>sweet |
| When can you fix it? | **Quand pouvez-vous le réparer?**<br>kahn poo·veh·voo ler reh·pah·reh |
| How much do I owe you? | **Combien vous dois-je?**<br>com·bee·an voo dwahsh |
| When is the garbage collected? | **Quand ramasse-t-on les ordures?**<br>kahn rah·mahs·tohn leh·zor·door |

## Likely Reactions

| | |
|---|---|
| What's your name? | **Comment vous appelez-vous?**<br>com·mahn voo·zah·pleh·voo |
| What's your address? | **Quelle est votre adresse?**<br>kel eh voht ah·dress |
| There's a store in town. | **Il y a un magasin en ville.**<br>il yah an mah·gah·zan ahn veel |
| There's a store in the village. | **Il y a un magasin dans le village.**<br>il yah an mah·gah·zan dahn ler<br>vee·lahsh |
| I can't come … | **Je ne peux pas venir…**<br>sher ner per pah ver·neer |
| … today. | **aujourd'hui.**<br>oh·shoor·dwee |
| … this week. | **cette semaine.**<br>set ser·men |
| … until Monday. | **avant lundi.**<br>ah·vahn lern·dee |

I can come …

**Je peux venir...**
sher per ver·neer

… on Tuesday.

**mardi.**
mar·dee

… when you want.

**quand vous voulez.**
kahn voo voo·leh

Every day.

**Tous les jours.**
too leh shoor

Every other day.

**Tous les deux jours.**
too leh der shoor

On Wednesdays.

**Le mercredi.**
ler mairk·rdee

For days of the week, see p. 116.

# General Shopping

## The Drugstore

### Essential Information

- Look for the word **Pharmacie** or the sign at right.

- Prescription medicines are available only at a drugstore.

- Some nonprescription drugs can be bought at a supermarket or department store, as well as at a drugstore.

- Try the drugstore before going to the doctor: Pharmacists are usually qualified to treat minor health problems.

- To claim money back on prescriptions when you return home, remove price labels from medicines and stick them on the prescription sheet.

- Drugstores take turns staying open all night and on Sundays. If a drugstore is closed, a notice on the door with the heading **Pharmacie de Garde** or **Pharmacie de Service** gives the address of the nearest drugstore that is open.

- Some toiletries can also be bought at a **parfumerie**, but they will probably be more expensive there.

- For finding a drugstore, see p. 10.

### What to Say

| | |
|---|---|
| I'd like … | **Je voudrais…**<br>sher voo·dreh |
| … some Alka Seltzer. | **de l'Alka Seltzer.**<br>der lahl·kah selt·ser |
| … some antiseptic. | **un antiseptique.**<br>an ahn·tee·sep·teek |
| … some aspirin. | **de l'aspirine.**<br>der lah·speer·een |
| … a bandage. | **une bande.**<br>oon bahnd |
| … some Band-Aids. | **du sparadrap.**<br>doo spah·rah·drah |
| … some cotton balls. | **du coton.**<br>doo coh·tohn |

I'd like …

Je voudrais…
sher voo·dreh

… some eyedrops.

**des gouttes pour les yeux.**
deh goot poor leh·zyer

… some foot powder.

**une poudre anti-perspirante.**
oon pood ahn·tee·pair·speer·ahnt

… some sterile gauze.

**de la gaze.**
der lah gahz

… some inhalant.

**un inhalateur.**
an een·ah·lah·ter

… some insect repellent.

**une crème anti-moustiques.**
oon crem ahn·tee·moo·steek

… some lip balm.

**du baume pour les lèvres.**
doo bohm poor leh lev

… some nose drops.

**des gouttes pour le nez.**
deh goot poor ler neh

… some throat lozenges.

**des pastilles pour la gorge.**
deh pah·stee poor lah gorsh

… some Vaseline.

**de la Vaseline.**
der lah vahs·leen

I'd like something for …

**Je voudrais un produit pour…**
sher voo·dreh an proh·dwee poor

… bites/stings.

**les piqûres.**
leh pee·koor

… burns.

**les brûlures.**
leh brool·yoor

… a cold.

**le rhume.**
ler room

… constipation.

**la constipation.**
lah con·stee·pah·syohn

… a cough.

**la toux.**
lah too

… diarrhea.

**la diarrhée.**
lah dee·ah·reh

… an earache.

**le mal d'oreille.**
ler mahl doh·ray

… flu.

**la grippe.**
lah greep

… sore gums.

**la gingivite.**
lah shan·shee·veet

… sprains.

**les entorses.**
leh·zahn·torss

… sunburn.

**les coups de soleil.**
leh coo der soh·lay

I'd like something for …

**Je voudrais un produit pour…**
sher voo·dreh an proh·dwee poor

… travel sickness.

**le mal de mer.**
ler mahl der mair

I'd like …

**Je voudrais…**
sher voo·dreh

… some baby food.

**de la nourriture pour bébés.**
der lah noo·ree·toor poor beh·beh

… some contraceptives.

**des contraceptives.**
deh cohn·trah·sep·teev

… some deodorant.

**un déodorant.**
an deh·oh·doh·rahn

… some disposable diapers.

**des couches en cellulose.**
deh coosh ahn sel·yoo·lohz

… some hand cream.

**de la crème pour les mains.**
der lah crem poor leh man

… some lipstick.

**du rouge à lèvres.**
doo roosh ah lev

… some make-up remover.

**un démaquillant.**
an deh·mah·kee·yahn

… some kleenex.

**des Kleenex.**
deh klee·nex

… some razor blades.

**des lames de rasoir.**
deh lahm der rah·zwah

… some safety pins.

**des épingles de sûreté.**
deh·zeh·pang der soor·teh

… some sanitary napkins.

**des serviettes périodiques.**
deh sair·vyet peh·ree·oh·deek

… some shaving cream.

**de la crème à raser.**
der lah crem ah rah·zeh

… some soap.

**du savon.**
doo sah·vohn

… some sunscreen.

**une crème solaire.**
oon crem soh·lair

… some talcum powder.

**du talc.**
doo tahlk

… some tampons.

**des Tampax.**
deh tahm·pahx

… some toilet paper.

**du papier hygiénique.**
doo pah·pyeh ee·shee·eh·neek

… some toothpaste.

**du dentifrice.**
doo dahn·tee·freess

For other essential expressions, see "Shop Talk," p. 44.

# Vacation Items

## Essential Information

• Here are other places to shop at and signs to look for.

| | |
|---|---|
| **Librairie—Papeterie** | Stationery/bookstore |
| **Bureau de Tabac** | Tobacco shop |
| **Cartes postales—Souvenirs** | Postcards and souvenirs |
| **Photographie** | Film and photography equipment |

• The main department stores in France are the following.

**Monoprix**
**Prisunic**
**Inno**

## What to Say

| | |
|---|---|
| Where can I buy …? | **Où puis-je acheter…?** |
| | oo pweesh ahsh·teh |
| I would like … | **Je voudrais…** |
| | sher voo·dreh |
| … a bag. | **un sac.** |
| | an sahk |
| … a beach ball. | **un ballon pour la plage.** |
| | an bah·lohn poor lah plahsh |
| … a bucket. | **un seau.** |
| | an soh |
| … some envelopes. | **des enveloppes.** |
| | deh·zahn·vlop |
| … a guidebook. | **un guide.** |
| | an gheed |
| … a handbag/purse. | **un sac à main.** |
| | an sahk ah man |
| … a map (of the area). | **une carte (de la région).** |
| | oon cart (der lah reh·shyohn) |
| … a newspaper in English. | **un journal anglais.** |
| | an shoor·nahl ahn·gleh |
| … a parasol. | **un parasol.** |
| | an pah·rah·sol |
| … some postcards. | **des cartes postales.** |
| | deh cart poh·stahl |
| … a shovel. | **une pelle.** |
| | oon pel |

| | |
|---|---|
| Where can I buy ...? | **Où puis-je acheter...?** |
| | oo pweesh ahsh·teh |
| I would like ... | **Je voudrais...** |
| | sher voo·dreh |
| ... a straw hat. | **un chapeau de paille.** |
| | an shah·poh der pye |
| ... a suitcase. | **une valise.** |
| | oon vah·leez |
| ... some sunglasses. | **des lunettes de soleil.** |
| | deh loo·net der soh·lay |
| ... an umbrella. | **un parapluie.** |
| | an pah·rah·plwee |
| ... some writing paper. | **du papier à lettres.** |
| | doo pah·pyeh ah let |
| I would like ... [*show the camera*] | **Je voudrais...** |
| | sher voo·dreh |
| ... a roll of color film ... | **un rouleau de pellicules couleur** |
| | an roo·loh der peh·lee·cool coo·ler |
| ... a roll of black and white film ... | **un rouleau de pellicules noir et blanc** |
| | an roo·loh der peh·lee·cool nwah eh blahn |
| ... for prints. | **pour photos.** |
| | poor foh·toh |
| ... for slides. | **pour diapositives.** |
| | poor dee·ah·poh·zee·teev |
| ... 12 (24/36) exposures. | **douze (vingt-quatre/trente-six) poses.** |
| | dooz (vant·cat/trahnt·see) pohz |
| ... some batteries. | **des piles.** |
| | deh peel |
| This camera is broken. | **Cet appareil ne marche plus.** |
| | set ah·pah·ray ner marsh ploo |
| The film is stuck. | **Le film est coincé.** |
| | ler feelm eh kwen·seh |
| Please, can you ... | **S'il vous plaît, pouvez-vous...** |
| | sil voo pleh poo·veh·voo |
| ... develop/print this? | **développer/tirer ceci?** |
| | deh·veh·loh·peh/tee·reh ser·see |
| ... load the camera for me? | **charger l'appareil?** |
| | shar·sheh lah·pah·ray |

For other essential expressions, see "Shop Talk," p. 44.

# The Tobacco Shop

## Essential Information

- Tobacco is sold only where you see the signs at right.

- A tobacco shop is called a **Bureau de Tabac**.

- For asking if there is a tobacco shop nearby, see p. 12.

- All tobacco shops sell postage stamps.

- A tobacco shop is sometimes part of a café (**Café-Tabac**), a stationery store (**Papeterie**), or a newsstand (**Tabac-Journaux**).

## What to Say

| | |
|---|---|
| A packet of cigarettes … | **Un paquet de cigarettes…**<br>an pah·keh der see·gah·ret |
| … with filters. | **à bout filtre.**<br>ah boo feelt |
| … without filters. | **sans filtre.**<br>sahn feelt |
| … king-size. | **longues.**<br>lohng |
| … menthol. | **à la menthe.**<br>ah lah mahnt |
| Those up there … | **Celles-là, en haut…**<br>sel·lah ahn oh |
| … on the right. | **à droite.**<br>ah drwaht |
| … on the left. | **à gauche.**<br>ah gohsh |
| These. [*point*] | **Celles-ci.**<br>sel·see |
| Cigarettes, please. | **Des cigarettes, s'il vous plaît.**<br>deh see·gah·ret sil voo pleh |
| 100, 200, 300 | **cent, deux cents, trois cents**<br>sahn, der sahn, trwah sahn |
| Two packs. | **Deux paquets.**<br>der pah·keh |

| | |
|---|---|
| Do you have … | **Avez-vous…**<br>ah·veh·voo |
| … American cigarettes? | **des cigarettes américaines?**<br>deh see·gah·ret ah·meh·ree·ken |
| … American pipe tobacco? | **du tabac de pipe américain?**<br>doo tah·bah der peep<br>ah·meh·ree·can |
| … rolling tobacco? | **du tabac à rouler?**<br>doo tah·bah ah roo·leh |
| … a packet of pipe tobacco? | **un paquet de tabac de pipe?**<br>an pah·keh der tah·bah der peep |
| That one down there … | **Celui-là, en bas…**<br>ser·lwee·lah ahn bah |
| … on the right. | **à droite.**<br>ah drwaht |
| … on the left. | **à gauche.**<br>ah gohsh |
| This one. [*point*] | **Celui-ci.**<br>ser·lwee·see |
| That one. [*point*] | **Celui-là.**<br>ser·lwee·lah |
| Those. [*point*] | **Ceux-là.**<br>ser·lah |
| A cigar. | **Un cigare.**<br>an see·gar |
| Some cigars. | **Des cigares.**<br>deh see·gar |
| A box of matches. | **Une boîte d'allumettes.**<br>oon bwaht dah·loo·met |
| A package of pipe-cleaners. | **Un paquet de cure-pipes.**<br>an pah·keh der coor·peep |
| A lighter. | **Un briquet.**<br>an bree·keh |

For other essential expressions, see "Shop Talk," p. 44.

# Buying Clothes

## Essential Information

· Look for the following signs.

| | |
|---|---|
| **Confection Dames** | Women's Clothes |
| **Confection Hommes** | Men's Clothes |
| **Chaussures** | Shoes |

· Don't buy clothing without being measured first or trying the item on.

· Don't rely solely on conversion charts of clothing sizes (see p. 127).

· If you are buying clothing for someone else, take his or her measurements with you.

· The department stores **Monprix** and **Prisunic** sell clothes and shoes.

## What to Say

| | |
|---|---|
| I would like … | **Je voudrais…** |
| | sher voo·dreh |
| … a bathing suit. | **un maillot de bain.** |
| | an mah·yoh der ban |
| … a belt. | **une ceinture.** |
| | oon sen·toor |
| … a bikini. | **un bikini.** |
| | an bee·kee·nee |
| … a blouse. | **un chemisier.** |
| | an sher·meez·yeh |
| … a bra. | **un soutien-gorge.** |
| | an soo·tyen·gorsh |
| … a cap (swimming/skiing). | **un bonnet (de bain/de ski).** |
| | an boh·neh (der ban/der skee) |
| … a cardigan. | **un cardigan.** |
| | an car·dee·gahn |
| … a coat. | **un manteau.** |
| | an mahn·toh |
| … a dress. | **une robe.** |
| | oon rohb |
| … a hat. | **un chapeau.** |
| | an shah·poh |
| … a jacket. | **une veste.** |
| | oon vest |

| | |
|---|---|
| I would like … | **Je voudrais…**<br>sher voo·dreh |
| … some jeans. | **un jean.**<br>an sheen |
| … a nightgown. | **une chemise de nuit.**<br>oon sher·meez der nwee |
| … some pajamas. | **un pyjama.**<br>an pee·shah·mah |
| … some pants. | **un pantalon.**<br>an pahn·tah·lohn |
| … a parka. | **un anorak.**<br>an ah·noh·rahk |
| … a raincoat. | **un imperméable.**<br>an am·pair·meh·ahb |
| … a (man's) shirt. | **une chemise.**<br>oon sher·meez |
| … some shorts. | **un short.**<br>an short |
| … a skirt. | **une jupe.**<br>oon shoop |
| … a (man's) suit. | **un costume.**<br>an coh·stoom |
| … a (woman's) suit. | **un tailleur.**<br>an tye·yer |
| … a sweater. | **un pull-over.**<br>an poo·loh·vair |
| … a T-shirt. | **un tee-shirt.**<br>an tee·shirt |
| … some tights. | **un collant.**<br>an coh·lahn |
| … some (men's) briefs. | **un slip.**<br>an sleep |
| … some (women's) briefs. | **une culotte.**<br>oon coo·lot |
| I would like a pair of … | **Je voudrais une paire de…**<br>sher voo·dreh oon pair der |
| … gloves. | **gants.**<br>gahn |
| … pantyhose. | **bas.**<br>bah |
| … socks. | **chaussettes.**<br>shoh·set |
| … shoes. | **chaussures.**<br>shoh·soor |

I would like a pair of …

**Je voudrais une paire de…**
sher voo·dreh oon pair der

… canvas shoes.

**chaussures en toile.**
shoh·soor ahn twahl

… sandals.

**sandales.**
sahn·dahl

… beach sandals.

**nu-pieds.**
noo·pee·eh

… dress shoes.

**chaussures habillées.**
shoh·soor ah·bee·yeh

… boots.

**bottes.**
bot

… moccasins/loafers.

**mocassins.**
moh·cah·san

My size is ….

**Je prends du….**
sher prahn doo

For numbers, see p. 112.

For clothing sizes, see p. 127.

Can you measure me, please?

**Pouvez-vous me mesurer,
s'il vous plaît?**
poo·veh·voo mer mer·zoo·reh
sil voo pleh

Can I try it on?

**Puis-je l'essayer?**
pweesh leh·seh·yeh

It's for a present.

**C'est pour un cadeau.**
seh poor an cah·doh

These are the
measurements …. [*show
written measurements*]

**Voici les mesures….**
vwah·see leh mer·zoor

collar

**tour de cou**
toor der coo

shoulders

**épaules**
eh·pohl

bust/chest

**poitrine**
pwah·treen

waist

**taille**
tye

hips

**hanches**
ahnsh

leg

**jambe**
shahmb

| | |
|---|---|
| Do you have something … | **Avez-vous quelque chose…** |
| | ah·veh·voo kel·ker shohz |
| … in black? | **en noir?** |
| | ahn nwah |
| … in blue? | **en bleu?** |
| | ahn bler |
| … in brown? | **en marron?** |
| | ahn mah·rohn |
| … in green? | **en vert?** |
| | ahn vair |
| … in gray? | **en gris?** |
| | ahn gree |
| … in pink? | **en rose?** |
| | ahn rohz |
| … in red? | **en rouge?** |
| | ahn roosh |
| … in white? | **en blanc?** |
| | ahn blahn |
| … in yellow? | **en jaune?** |
| | ahn shohn |
| … in this color? [*point*] | **de cette couleur?** |
| | der set coo·ler |
| … in cotton? | **en coton?** |
| | ahn coh·tohn |
| … in denim? | **en toile?** |
| | ahn twahl |
| … in leather? | **en cuir?** |
| | ahn kweer |
| … in nylon? | **en nylon?** |
| | ahn nee·lohn |
| … in suede? | **en daim?** |
| | ahn dam |
| … in wool? | **en laine?** |
| | ahn len |
| … in this material? [*point*] | **dans ce tissu?** |
| | dahn ser tee·soo |

For other essential expressions, see "Shop Talk," p. 44.

# Replacing Equipment

## Essential Information

· Look for the following shops and signs.

| | |
|---|---|
| **Quincaillerie** | Hardware |
| **Électroménager** | Electrical items |
| **Droguerie** | Store selling household goods and household cleaning materials |

· In a supermarket, look for this display: **Entretien**.

· For asking directions to a shop, see p. 10.

· At a campsite, try its shop first.

## What to Say

Do you have …
**Avez-vous…**
ah·veh·voo

… an adapter? [*show appliance*]
**un adaptateur?**
an ah·dahp·tah·ter

… a bottle opener?
**un ouvre-bouteille?**
an oov·boo·tay

… a can opener?
**un ouvre-boîte?**
an oov·bwaht

… a clothesline?
**une corde à linge?**
oon cord ah lansh

… a corkscrew?
**un tire-bouchon?**
an teer·boo·shohn

… any detergent?
**de la lessive?**
der lah leh·seev

… any dish detergent?
**du liquide pour la vaisselle?**
doo lee·keed poor lah veh·sel

… a dish towel?
**un torchon?**
an tor·shohn

… any disinfectant?
**un désinfectant?**
an deh·zan·fek·tahn

… any disposable cups?
**des gobelets à jeter?**
deh gohb·leh ah sher·teh

… any disposable plates?
**des assiettes à jeter?**
deh·zah·syet ah sher·teh

… a flashlight?
**une lampe de poche?**
oon lahmp der pohsh

… any flashlight batteries?
**des piles pour lampe de poche?**
deh peel poor lahmp der pohsh

| | |
|---|---|
| Do you have … | **Avez-vous…** |
| | ah·veh·voo |
| … any forks? | **des fourchettes?** |
| | deh foor·shet |
| … a fuse? [*show the one to be replaced*] | **un fusible?** |
| | an foo·zeeb |
| … insecticide? | **une bombe insecticide?** |
| | oon bomb an·sek·tee·seed |
| … any knives? | **des couteaux?** |
| | deh coo·toh |
| … a light bulb? [*show the one to be replaced*] | **une ampoule?** |
| | oon ahm·pool |
| … any paper towels? | **du essuie-tout?** |
| | doo es·wee·too |
| … a plastic bucket? | **un seau en plastique?** |
| | an soh ahn plah·steek |
| … a scouring pad? | **un tampon pour récurer?** |
| | an tahm·pohn poor reh·coo·reh |
| … a sponge? | **une éponge?** |
| | oon eh·ponsh |
| … any string? | **de la ficelle?** |
| | der lah fee·sel |
| … any tent pegs? | **des piquets de tente?** |
| | deh pee·keh der tahnt |
| … a universal plug (for the sink)? | **un tampon universel (pour évier)?** |
| | an tahm·pohn oo·nee·vair·sel (poor eh·vyeh) |
| … a wrench? | **une clé plate?** |
| | oon cleh plaht |

For other essential expressions, see "Shop Talk," p. 44.

# Shop Talk

## Essential Information

- France uses euro currency. Information is given below for coins and bills.

  Coins   1, 2, 5, 10, 20, and 50 cents; 1 and 2 euros
  Bills    €5, €10, €20, €50, €100, €200, €500

## CURRENCY CONVERTER

- Since the relative strengths of currencies vary, we cannot provide accurate exchange rates here. However, by filling in the charts below prior to your trip, you can create a handy currency converter.

| DOLLARS | EUROS | EUROS | DOLLARS |
|---------|-------|-------|---------|
| 1 | _____ | 1 | _____ |
| 2 | _____ | 2 | _____ |
| 3 | _____ | 3 | _____ |
| 4 | _____ | 4 | _____ |
| 5 | _____ | 5 | _____ |
| 10 | _____ | 10 | _____ |
| 15 | _____ | 15 | _____ |
| 25 | _____ | 25 | _____ |
| 50 | _____ | 50 | _____ |
| 75 | _____ | 75 | _____ |
| 100 | _____ | 100 | _____ |
| 250 | _____ | 250 | _____ |

- Important weights and measures follow.

| | | |
|---|---|---|
| 50 grams | **cinquante grammes** | |
| | san·kahnt grahm | |
| 100 grams | **cent grammes** | |
| | sahn grahm | |
| 200 grams | **deux cents grammes** | |
| | der sahn grahm | |
| ½ kilo | **un demi-kilo** | |
| | an der·mee·kee·loh | |

| | |
|---|---|
| 1 kilo | **un kilo** |
| | an kee·loh |
| 2 kilos | **deux kilos** |
| | der kee·loh |
| ½ liter | **un demi-litre** |
| | an der·mee·leet |
| 1 liter | **un litre** |
| | an leet |
| 2 liters | **deux litres** |
| | der leet |

For numbers, see p. 112.

- In some small stores, don't be surprised if customers, as well as the shop assistants, say "hello" and "good-bye" to you.

## What to Say

### CUSTOMER

| | |
|---|---|
| Hello./Good morning./ Good day./Good afternoon. | **Bonjour.** bohn·shoor |
| Good-bye. | **Au revoir.** oh reh·vwah |
| I'm just looking. | **Je regarde.** sher rer·gard |
| Excuse me. | **Pardon.** par·dohn |
| How much is this/that? | **C'est combien, ça?** seh com·bee·an sah |
| What is that?/What are those? | **Qu'est-ce que c'est ça?** kes ker seh sah |
| Is there a discount? | **Est-ce que vous faites une remise?** es ker voo fet oon rer·meez |
| I'd like that, please. | **Je voudrais ça, s'il vous plaît.** sher voo·dreh sah sil voo pleh |
| Not that. | **Pas ça.** pah sah |
| Like that. | **Comme ça.** com sah |
| That's enough, thank you. | **Ça suffit, merci.** sah soo·fee mair·see |
| More, please. | **Encore un peu, s'il vous plaît.** ahn·cor an per sil voo pleh |
| Less, please. | **Moins, s'il vous plaît.** mwen sil voo pleh |

| | |
|---|---|
| That's fine./Okay. | **Ça va.**<br>sah vah |
| I'm not going to take it,<br>thank you. | **Merci, je ne le prends pas.**<br>mair·see sher ner ler prahn pah |
| It's not right. | **Ça ne va pas.**<br>sah ner vah pah |
| Thank you very much. | **Merci bien.**<br>mair·see bee·an |
| Do you have something … | **Avez-vous quelque chose…**<br>ah·veh·voo kel·ker shohz |
| … better? | **de mieux?**<br>der mee·er |
| … cheaper? | **de moins cher?**<br>der mwen shair |
| … different? | **de différent?**<br>der dee·feh·rahn |
| … larger? | **de plus grand?**<br>der ploo grahn |
| … smaller? | **de plus petit?**<br>der ploo ptee |
| (At) what time do you … | **À quelle heure…**<br>ah kel er |
| … open? | **ouvrez-vous?**<br>oo·vreh·voo |
| … close? | **fermez-vous?**<br>fair·meh·voo |
| Can I have a bag, please? | **Puis-je avoir un sac, s'il vous plaît?**<br>pweesh ah·vwah an sahk sil voo<br>pleh |
| Can I have a receipt? | **Puis-je avoir un reçu?**<br>pweesh ah·vwah an rer·soo |
| Do you take … | **Acceptez-vous…**<br>ahk·sep·teh·voo |
| … American money? | **l'argent américain?**<br>lar·shahn ah·meh·ree·can |
| … traveler's checks? | **les chèques-voyage?**<br>leh shek vwah·yahsh |
| … credit cards? | **la carte bleue?**<br>lah cart bler |

| | |
|---|---|
| I would like … | **J'en voudrais…**<br>shahn voo·dreh |
| … one like that. | **un comme ça.**<br>an com sah |
| … two like that. | **deux comme ça.**<br>der com sah |

### SHOP ASSISTANT

| | |
|---|---|
| Can I help you? | **Qu'y a-t-il pour votre service?**<br>kee ah·teel poor voht sair·veess |
| What would you like? | **Vous désirez?**<br>voo deh·zee·reh |
| Will that be all? | **Ce sera tout?**<br>ser ser·rah too |
| Is that all? | **C'est tout?**<br>seh too |
| Anything else? | **Vous désirez autre chose?**<br>voo deh·zee·reh oht shohz |
| Would you like it wrapped? | **Je vous l'enveloppe?**<br>sher voo lahn·vlop |
| I'm sorry, there are none left. | **Je regrette, il n'y en a plus.**<br>sher rer·gret il nee ahn ah ploo |
| I don't have any. | **Je n'en ai pas.**<br>sher nah·neh pah |
| I don't have any more. | **Je n'en ai plus.**<br>sher nah·neh ploo |
| How many do you want?/<br>  How much do you want? | **Vous en voulez combien?**<br>voo·zahn voo·leh com·bee·an |
| Is that enough? | **Ça suffit?**<br>sah soo·fee |

# Shopping for Food

## Bread

### Essential Information

- For finding a bakery, see p. 10.
- Here are key words to look for.

  | | |
  |---|---|
  | **Boulangerie** | Bakery |
  | **Boulanger** | Baker |
  | **Pain** | Bread |

- Nearly all supermarkets and general stores sell bread.
- Small bakeries are usually open between 7:30 A.M. and 7:00–8:00 P.M. Most close on Mondays and public holidays but are open on Sundays until 1:00 P.M.
- The most characteristic type of loaf is the baguette, which comes in a number of sizes.
- For any other type of loaf, just ask for **un pain** and point.

### What to Say

| | |
|---|---|
| Some bread, please. | **Du pain, s'il vous plaît.**<br>doo pan sil voo pleh |
| A loaf (like that). | **Un pain (comme ça).**<br>an pan (com sah) |
| A baguette. | **Une baguette.**<br>oon bah·get |
| A large one. | **Une grande.**<br>oon grahnd |
| A long, thin one. | **Une ficelle.**<br>oon fee·sel |
| Half a baguette. | **Une demi-baguette.**<br>oon der·mee·bah·get |
| A brown loaf. | **Un pain intégral.**<br>an pan an·teh·grahl |
| A bread roll. | **Un petit pain.**<br>an ptee pan |
| A croissant. | **Un croissant.**<br>an crwah·sahn |
| A brioche. | **Une brioche.**<br>oon bree·ohsh |

| A sweet bun with raisins. | **Un pain aux raisins.** |
| | an pan oh reh·zan |
| A chocolate-filled bun. | **Un pain au chocolat.** |
| | an pan oh shoh·coh·lah |
| Two loaves. | **Deux pains.** |
| | der pan |
| Two baguettes. | **Deux baguettes.** |
| | der bah·get |
| Four rolls. | **Quatre petits pains.** |
| | kat ptee pan |
| Four croissants. | **Quatre croissants.** |
| | kat crwah·sahn |

For other essential expressions, see "Shop Talk," p. 44.

# Cakes

## Essential Information

· Here are key words to look for.

| **Pâtisserie** | Pastry shop |
| **Pâtissier** | Cake and pastry maker |
| **Pâtisseries** | Pastries or cakes |

· **Pâtisseries** generally keep the same hours as small bakeries (see p. 48).

· **Salon de thé**: a room, usually off a **pâtisserie**, where customers sit at tables and are served cakes, ice cream, soft drinks, tea, coffee, or chocolate. For ordering a drink, see p. 67.

· For finding a bakery, see p. 10.

## What to Say

The type of cakes you find in the shops varies from region to region, but the most common ones are listed below.

| an éclair | **un éclair** |
| | an eh·clair |
| a pastry filled with vanilla cream | **un chou à la crème** |
| | an shoo ah lah crem |
| a pastry with coffee cream filling (literally, a nun) | **une religieuse** |
| | oon reh·lee·shee·erz |
| a rum baba | **un baba au rhum** |
| | an bah·bah oh room |

| | |
|---|---|
| layers of puff pastry and almond cream | **un millefeuille** an meel·fer·ee |
| an apple turnover | **un chausson aux pommes** an shoh·sohn oh pom |
| a doughnut | **un pet de nonne** an peh der non |
| a small ... tart | **une tartelette...** oon tart·let |
| ... apple ... | **aux pommes** oh pom |
| ... strawberry ... | **aux fraises** oh frez |
| ... apricot ... | **aux abricots** oh·zah·bree·coh |

You usually ask for medium-sized cakes by the number you wish to buy.

| | |
|---|---|
| Two doughnuts, please. | **Deux pets de nonne, s'il vous plaît.** der peh der non sil voo pleh |
| Half a dozen cream cakes. | **Une demi-douzaine de gâteaux à la crème.** oon der·mee·doo·zen der gah·toh ah lah crem |

Small cakes are bought by weight, and it is best to point to the selection you prefer.

| | |
|---|---|
| 200 grams of petits fours. | **Deux cents grammes de petits fours.** der sahn grahm der ptee foor |
| 400 grams of cookies. | **Quatre cents grammes de biscuits.** kat sahn grahm der bee·skwee |

You may want to buy larger cakes by the slice.

| | |
|---|---|
| One slice of apple cake. | **Une tranche de gâteaux aux pommes.** oon trahnsh der gah·toh oh pom |
| Two slices of almond cake. | **Deux tranches de gâteaux aux amandes.** der trahnsh der gah·toh oh·zah·mahnd |

You may also want to ask for a variety of pastries.

| | |
|---|---|
| A selection, please. | **Mélangés, s'il vous plaît.** meh·lahn·sheh sil voo pleh |

For other essential expressions, see "Shop Talk," p. 44.

# Ice Cream and Candy

## Essential Information

- Here are key words to look for.

| | |
|---|---|
| **Glaces** | Ice cream |
| **Glacier** | Ice-cream maker/seller |
| **Confiserie** | Candy shop |
| **Confiseur** | Candy maker/seller |
| **Pâtissier** | Cake and pastry maker |

- The best-known ice-cream brand names in France are the following.

**Frigécrème**
**Gervais**
**Miko**
**Motta**
**Ski**

- Prepackaged candy is available in general stores and supermarkets.

## What to Say

| | |
|---|---|
| A … ice cream, please. | **Une glace…, s'il vous plaît.** |
| | oon glahss… sil voo pleh |
| … banana … | **à la banane** |
| | ah lah bah·nahn |
| … chocolate … | **au chocolat** |
| | oh shoh·coh·lah |
| … coffee … | **au moka** |
| | oh moh·kah |
| … pistachio … | **à la pistache** |
| | ah lah pee·stahsh |
| … raspberry … | **à la framboise** |
| | ah lah frahm·bwahz |
| … strawberry … | **à la fraise** |
| | ah lah frez |
| … vanilla … | **à la vanille** |
| | ah lah vah·nee |
| Two euros' worth. | **Deux euros.** |
| | der er·oh |
| A single cone. | **Un cornet simple.** |
| | an cor·neh samp |
| Two single cones. | **Deux cornets simples.** |
| | der cor·neh samp |

| | |
|---|---|
| A double-dip cone. | **Un cornet double.**<br>an cor·neh doob |
| Two double-dip cones. | **Deux cornets doubles.**<br>der cor·neh doob |
| A mixed cone. | **Un cornet mélangé.**<br>an cor·neh meh·lahn·sheh |
| A carton. | **Un carton.**<br>an car·tohn |
| A lollipop. | **Une sucette.**<br>oon soo·set |
| A packet of … | **Un paquet de…**<br>an pah·keh der |
| 100 grams of … | **Cent grammes de…**<br>sahn grahm der |
| 200 grams of … | **Deux cents grammes de…**<br>der sahn grahm der |
| … candy. | **bonbons.**<br>bohn·bohn |
| … chocolates. | **chocolats.**<br>shoh·coh·lah |
| … mints. | **bonbons à la menthe.**<br>bohn·bohn ah lah mahnt |
| … toffees. | **caramels.**<br>cah·rah·mel |

For other essential expressions, see "Shop Talk," p. 44.

# In the Supermarket

### Essential Information

· Here are key words to look for.

| | |
|---|---|
| **Supermarché** | Supermarket |
| **Hypermarché** | Superstore |
| **Supérette** | Corner store |
| **Alimentation générale** | General food store |

· Here are some common signs at supermarkets.

| | |
|---|---|
| **Entrée** | Entrance |
| **Entrée interdite** | No entry |
| **Sortie** | Exit |
| **Sortie interdite** | No exit |
| **Sans issue** | No exit |
| **Sortie sans achats** | Exit without purchases |

| Caisse | Checkout, cashier |
|--------|-------------------|
| **Caisse rapide** | Express checkout |
| **En réclame** | Sale |
| **Libre service** | Self-service |
| **Chariots** | Carts |

- Opening times may vary, but most stores are open between 8:00 A.M. and 7:00 P.M. Superstores will often remain open until 10:00 P.M. Remember, however, that a great many stores are closed on Mondays, or at least on Monday mornings.

- It is usually not necessary to say anything in a supermarket, but you should ask if you don't see what you want.

- For non-food items, see "Replacing Equipment," p. 42.

### What to Say

| | |
|---|---|
| Excuse me, please. | **Pardonnez-moi, s'il vous plaît.**<br>par·doh·neh·mwah sil voo pleh |
| Where is … | **Où est…**<br>oo eh |
| … the bread? | **le pain?**<br>ler pan |
| … the butter? | **le beurre?**<br>ler ber |
| … the cheese? | **le fromage?**<br>ler froh·mahsh |
| … the chocolate? | **le chocolat?**<br>ler shoh·coh·lah |
| … the coffee? | **le café?**<br>ler cah·feh |
| … the cooking oil? | **l'huile?**<br>lweel |
| … the fresh fish? | **le poisson?**<br>ler pwah·sohn |
| … the canned fish? | **le poisson en conserve?**<br>ler pwah·son ahn cohn·sairv |
| … the jam? | **la confiture?**<br>lah cohn·fee·toor |
| … the meat? | **la viande?**<br>lah vee·ahnd |
| … the milk? | **le lait?**<br>ler leh |
| … the mineral water? | **l'eau minérale?**<br>loh mee·neh·rahl |

| | |
|---|---|
| Excuse me, please. | **Pardonnez-moi, s'il vous plaît.** |
| | par·doh·neh·mwah sil voo pleh |
| Where is … | **Où est…** |
| | oo eh |
| … the salt? | **le sel?** |
| | ler sel |
| … the sugar? | **le sucre?** |
| | ler sook |
| … the tea? | **le thé?** |
| | ler teh |
| … the vinegar? | **le vinaigre?** |
| | ler vee·neg |
| … the wine? | **le vin?** |
| | ler van |
| Where is/are … | **Où sont…** |
| | oo sohn |
| … the candy? | **les bonbons?** |
| | leh bohn·bohn |
| … the cookies? | **les biscuits?** |
| | leh bee·skwee |
| … the eggs? | **les œufs?** |
| | leh·zerf |
| … the frozen foods? | **les produits surgelés?** |
| | leh proh·dwee soorsh·leh |
| … the fruit? | **les fruits?** |
| | leh frwee |
| … the canned fruit? | **les fruits en conserve?** |
| | leh frwee ahn cohn·sairv |
| … the fruit juices? | **les jus de fruits?** |
| | leh shoo der frwee |
| … the pasta? | **les pâtes?** |
| | leh paht |
| … the potato chips? | **les pommes chips?** |
| | leh pom sheep |
| … the seafood? | **les fruits de mer?** |
| | leh frwee der mair |
| … the snails? | **les escargots?** |
| | leh·zeh·scar·goh |
| … the soft drinks? | **les boissons?** |
| | leh bwah·sohn |
| … the vegetables? | **les légumes?** |
| | leh leh·goom |
| … the canned vegetables? | **les légumes en conserve?** |
| | leh leh·goom ahn cohn·sairv |

Where is/are …

**Où sont…**
oo sohn

… the yogurt?

**les yaourts?**
leh yah·oor

For other essential expressions, see "Shop Talk," p. 44.

# Picnic Food

## Essential Information

· Here are key words to look for.

| | |
|---|---|
| **Charcuterie** | Delicatessen, pork butcher shop |
| **Traiteur** | Delicatessen |
| **Charcutier** | Pork butcher |

· In these shops, you can buy a wide variety of food, such as ham, salami, cheese, olives, appetizers, sausages, and freshly made carry-out dishes. Specialties vary from region to region.

· Here's a guide to the amount of prepared salad to buy.

2–3 ounces/70 grams per person, if eaten as an appetizer
to a substantial meal
3–4 ounces/100 grams per person, if eaten as the main course
of a picnic-style meal

## What to Say

A slice of …

**Une tranche de…**
oon trahnsh der

Two slices of …

**Deux tranches de…**
der trahnsh der

… garlic sausage.

**saucisson à l'ail.**
soh·see·sohn ah lye

… cooked ham.

**jambon cuit.**
shahm·bohn kwee

… cured ham.

**jambon cru.**
shahm·bohn croo

… pâté.

**pâté.**
pah·teh

… roast beef.

**rôti de bœuf.**
roh·tee der berf

… roast pork.

**rôti de porc.**
roh·tee der por

| | |
|---|---|
| Two slices of … | **Deux tranches de…**<br>der trahnsh der |
| … salami. | **saucisson.**<br>soh·see·sohn |
| 100 grams of … | **Cent grammes de…**<br>sahn grahm der |
| 150 grams of … | **Cent cinquante grammes de…**<br>sahn san·kahnt grahm der |
| 200 grams of … | **Deux cents grammes de…**<br>der sahn grahm der |
| 300 grams of … | **Trois cents grammes de…**<br>trwah sahn grahm der |
| … Russian salad. | **salade russe.**<br>sah·lahd rooss |
| … tomato salad. | **salade de tomates.**<br>sah·lahd der toh·maht |
| … cheese. | **fromage.**<br>froh·mahsh |
| 100 grams … | **Cent grammes…**<br>sahn grahm |
| … of olives. | **d'olives.**<br>doh·leev |
| … of anchovies. | **d'anchois.**<br>dahn·shwah |

You might also like to try some of the following foods.

| | |
|---|---|
| tripe sausage | **andouille**<br>ahn·doo·ee |
| boat-shaped pastry with<br>shrimp filling | **barquette de crevettes**<br>bar·ket der crer·vet |
| diced beef cooked with wine<br>and mushrooms | **bœuf aux champignons**<br>berf oh shahm·pee·nyohn |
| diced beef cooked with wine<br>and olives | **bœuf aux olives**<br>berf oh·zoh·leev |
| diced beef cooked in a thick<br>wine sauce | **bœuf en daube**<br>berf ahn dohb |
| vol-au-vent shell filled with<br>sweetbreads and mushrooms<br>in a cream sauce | **bouchée à la reine**<br>boo·shay ah lah ren |
| black pudding | **boudin**<br>boo·dan |
| salt cod mixed with oil, cream,<br>and garlic | **brandade de morue**<br>brahn·dahd der moh·roo |

| | |
|---|---|
| mushrooms cooked with wine, tomatoes, and spices | **champignons à la grecque** <br> shahm·pee·nyohn ah lah grek |
| artichoke hearts | **cœurs d'artichaut** <br> ker dar·tee·shoh |
| diced vegetables in mayonnaise | **macédoine de légumes** <br> mah·seh·dwan der leh·goom |
| hard-boiled eggs with mayonnaise | **œufs mayonnaise** <br> erf mye·oh·nez |
| quiche with ham or bacon | **quiche lorraine** <br> keesh loh·ren |
| pork sausage served in a tureen | **rillettes** <br> ree·yet |
| pastry with creamy cheese filling | **rouleau au fromage** <br> roo·loh oh froh·mahsh |
| salad of tomato, potato, egg, anchovy, tuna fish, and olives in oil and vinegar | **salade niçoise** <br> sah·lahd nee·swahz |
| frankfurter | **saucisse de Strasbourg** <br> soh·seess der strahs·boor |
| smoked garlic sausage | **saucisson sec** <br> soh·see·sohn sek |
| onion pie | **tarte à l'oignon** <br> tart ah loh·nyohn |
| cheese pie | **tarte au fromage** <br> tart oh froh·mahsh |
| stuffed tomatoes | **tomates farcies** <br> toh·maht far·see |
| creamy white cheese | **Brie** <br> bree |
| full, fat soft white cheese | **Camembert** <br> cah·mahm·bair |
| Swiss cheese with big holes | **Emmental** <br> em·mahn·tahl |
| goat's cheese | **fromage de chèvre** <br> froh·mahsh der shev |
| Swiss cheese, smooth in texture | **Gruyère** <br> groo·yair |
| soft cheese with holes | **Pont l'Évêque** <br> pohn leh·vek |
| strong, bluish cheese | **Roquefort** <br> rock·for |

For other essential expressions, see "Shop Talk," p. 44.

# Fruits and Vegetables

## Essential Information

- Here are key words to look for.

  | | |
  |---|---|
  | **Fruits** | Fruit |
  | **Légumes** | Vegetables |
  | **Primeurs** | Fresh fruit and vegetables |
  | **Fruitier** | Fruit seller |
  | **Marché** | Market |

- If possible, buy fruit and vegetables at a market, where they are cheaper and fresher than in stores and shops. Open-air markets are held once or twice a week in most areas (sometimes daily in large towns), usually in the mornings.

- It is customary for you to choose your own fruit and vegetables at the market (and in some shops) and for the attendant to weigh and price them. If convenient, take your own plastic, cloth, or string bag when shopping. Sturdy bags are not normally provided.

- Weight guide: One kilo of potatoes serves six people.

## What to Say

| | |
|---|---|
| 250 grams of … | **Deux cents cinquante grammes de…** <br> der sahn san·kahnt grahm der |
| ½ kilo (about 1 pound) of … | **Un demi-kilo de…** <br> an der·mee·kee·loh der |
| 1 kilo of … | **Un kilo de…** <br> an kee·loh der |
| 2 kilos of … | **Deux kilos de…** <br> der kee·loh der |
| … apples. | **pommes.** <br> pom |
| … bananas. | **bananes.** <br> bah·nahn |
| … cherries. | **cerises.** <br> seh·reez |
| … grapes (white/black). | **raisins (blancs/noirs).** <br> reh·zan (blahn/nwah) |
| … peaches. | **pêches.** <br> pesh |
| … pears. | **poires.** <br> pwahr |

| | |
|---|---|
| 250 grams of … | **Deux cents cinquante grammes de…** <br> der sahn san·kahnt grahm der |
| ½ kilo (about 1 pound) of … | **Un demi-kilo de…** <br> an der·mee·kee·loh der |
| 1 kilo of … | **Un kilo de…** <br> an kee·loh der |
| 2 kilos of … | **Deux kilos de…** <br> der kee·loh der |
| … plums. | **prunes.** <br> proon |
| … strawberries. | **fraises.** <br> frez |
| 1 kilo of oranges. | **Un kilo d'oranges.** <br> an kee·loh doh·rahnsh |
| A grapefruit, please. | **Un pamplemousse, s'il vous plaît.** <br> an pahmp·mooss sil voo pleh |
| A melon. | **Un melon.** <br> an mer·lohn |
| A pineapple. | **Un ananas.** <br> an ah·nah·nah |
| A watermelon. | **Une pastèque.** <br> oon pahs·tek |
| 250 grams of … | **Deux cents cinquante grammes de…** <br> der sahn san·kahnt grahm der |
| ½ kilo (about 1 pound) of … | **Un demi-kilo de…** <br> an der·mee·kee·loh der |
| 1 kilo of … | **Un kilo de…** <br> an kee·loh der |
| 2 kilos of … | **Deux kilos de…** <br> der kee·loh der |
| … carrots. | **carottes.** <br> cah·rot |
| … leeks. | **poireaux.** <br> pwah·roh |
| … mushrooms. | **champignons.** <br> shahm·pee·nyohn |
| … peas. | **petits pois.** <br> ptee pwah |
| … peppers (green/red). | **poivrons (verts/rouges).** <br> pwah·vrohn (vair/roosh) |
| … potatoes. | **pommes de terre.** <br> pom der tair |

250 grams of …
**Deux cents cinquante grammes de…**
der sahn san·kahnt grahm der

½ kilo (about 1 pound) of …
**Un demi-kilo de…**
an der·mee·kee·loh der

1 kilo of …
**Un kilo de…**
an kee·loh der

2 kilos of …
**Deux kilos de…**
der kee·loh der

… tomatoes.
**tomates.**
toh·maht

1 kilo …
**Un kilo…**
an kee·loh

… of asparagus.
**d'asperges.**
dah·spairsh

… of green beans.
**d'haricots verts.**
dah·ree·coh vair

… of onions.
**d'oignons.**
doh·nyohn

… of shallots.
**d'échalotes.**
deh·shah·lot

… of spinach.
**d'épinards.**
deh·pee·nar

A bunch of parsley.
**Un bouquet de persil.**
an boo·keh der pair·see

A bunch of radishes.
**Une botte de radis.**
oon bot der rah·dee

A head of garlic.
**Une tête d'ail.**
oon tet dye

A head of lettuce.
**Une salade.**
oon sah·lahd

A head of cauliflower.
**Un chou-fleur.**
an shoo·fler

A head of cabbage.
**Un chou.**
an shoo

A bunch of celery.
**Un pied de céleri.**
an pee·eh der seh·leh·ree

A cucumber.
**Un concombre.**
an cohn·comb

Like that, please.
**Comme ça, s'il vous plaît.**
com sah sil voo pleh

The following vegetables may not be familiar to you.

| eggplant | **aubergines** |
| | oh·bair·sheen |
| sea-kale | **blettes** |
| | blet |
| zucchini | **courgette** |
| | coor·shet |
| fennel | **fenouil** |
| | fer·noo·ee |

For other essential expressions, see "Shop Talk," p. 44.

# Meat

· Here are key words to look for.

| **Boucherie** | Butcher shop |
| **Boucher** | Butcher |

· Weight guide: 4–6 ounces/110–170 grams of meat serves one person.

· The figures on the following page can help you make sense of labels on counters and supermarket displays. Translations are often unhelpful, and you won't need to say the French word.

## What to Say

To buy a roast, first indicate the type of meat, then say how many people it is for.

| Some beef, please. | **Du bœuf, s'il vous plaît.** |
| | doo berf sil voo pleh |
| Some lamb. | **De l'agneau.** |
| | der lah·nyoh |
| Some mutton. | **Du mouton.** |
| | doo moo·tohn |
| Some pork. | **Du porc.** |
| | doo por |
| Some veal. | **Du veau.** |
| | doo voh |
| A roast … | **Un rôti…** |
| | an roh·tee |
| … for two people. | **pour deux personnes.** |
| | poor der pair·son |
| … for four people. | **pour quatre personnes.** |
| | poor kat pair·son |

Beef **Bœuf**

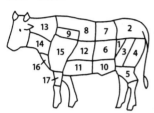

| | |
|---|---|
| 1 **Aiguillette baronne** | 10 **Flanchet** |
| 2 **Romsteck** | 11 **Tendron** |
| 3 **Tranche grasse** | 12 **Plat de côtes** |
| 4 **Gîte à la noix** | 13 **Second talon** |
| 5 **Gîte-gîte** | 14 **Veine grasse** |
| 6 **Bavette (pot-au-feu)** | 15 **Macreuse** |
| 7 **Contre-filet** | 16 **Poitrine** |
| 8 **Entrecôtes** | 17 **Gîte-gîte** |
| 9 **Paleron** | |

Veal **Veau**

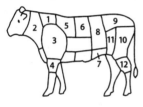

| | |
|---|---|
| 1 **Côtes découvertes** | 7 **Flanchet** |
| 2 **Collier** | 8 **Longe** |
| 3 **Épaule** | 9 **Quasi** |
| 4 **Jarret de devant** | 10 **Sous-noix** |
| 5 **Côtes secondes** | 11 **Noix pâtissière** |
| 6 **Côtes premières** | 12 **Jarret** |

Pork **Porc**

| | |
|---|---|
| 1 **Filet** | 7 **Échine** |
| 2 **Pointe** | 8 **Tête** |
| 3 **Jambon** | 9 **Épaule** |
| 4 **Ventre** | 10 **Jambonneau** |
| 5 **Côtes premières** | 11 **Poitrine** |
| 6 **Côtes découvertes** | |

Mutton **Mouton**

| |
|---|
| 1 **Côtes premières** |
| 2 **Selle** |
| 3 **Filet** |
| 4 **Gigot** |
| 5 **Haut de côtelettes** |
| 6 **Côtes secondes** |
| 7 **Côtes découvertes** |
| 8 **Collier** |
| 9 **Épaule** |
| 10 **Poitrine** |

| | |
|---|---|
| A roast … | **Un rôti…** |
| | an roh·tee |
| … for six people. | **pour six personnes.** |
| | poor see pair·son |
| Some steak, please. | **Du bifteck, s'il vous plaît.** |
| | doo beef·tek sil voo pleh |
| Some liver. | **Du foie.** |
| | doo fwah |
| Some kidneys. | **Des rognons.** |
| | deh roh·nyohn |
| Some heart. | **Du cœur.** |
| | doo ker |
| Some sausages. | **Des saucisses.** |
| | deh soh·seess |
| Ground beef … | **Bœuf haché…** |
| | berf ah·sheh |
| … for three people. | **pour trois personnes.** |
| | poor trwah pair·son |
| … for five people. | **pour cinq personnes.** |
| | poor sank pair·son |

For chops, order in the following way.

| | |
|---|---|
| Two veal chops. | **Deux escalopes de veau.** |
| | der·zeh·scah·lop der voh |
| Three pork chops. | **Trois côtelettes de porc.** |
| | trwah coht·let der por |
| Four lamb chops. | **Quatre côtelettes d'agneau.** |
| | kat coht·let dah·nyoh |
| Five mutton chops. | **Cinq côtelettes de mouton.** |
| | sank coht·let der moo·tohn |

You may also want the following.

| | |
|---|---|
| A chicken. | **Un poulet.** |
| | an poo·leh |
| A rabbit. | **Un lapin.** |
| | an lah·pan |
| A tongue. | **Une langue.** |
| | oon lahng |

For other essential expressions, see "Shop Talk," p. 44.

| | |
|---|---|
| Please can you … | **S'il vous plaît, pouvez-vous…** |
| | sil voo pleh poo·veh·voo |
| … grind it? | **le hacher?** |
| | ler ah·sheh |

| | |
|---|---|
| Please can you … | **S'il vous plaît, pouvez-vous…**<br>sil voo pleh poo·veh·voo |
| … dice it? | **le découper en dés?**<br>ler deh·coo·peh ahn deh |
| … trim the fat? | **enlever le gras?**<br>ahn·ler·veh ler grah |

# Fish

## Essential Information

- Look for the following sign.

  **Poissonnerie**   Fish market

- Another key phrase to look for is **Fruits de mer** (seafood).

- Markets and larger supermarkets usually have a fresh fish department.

- Weight guide: A minimum of 9 ounces/250 grams of fish on the bone serves one person. Use the following table as a guide.

  | | |
  |---|---|
  | 1/2 kilo/500 grams | for 2 people |
  | 1 kilo | for 4 people |
  | 1 1/2 kilo | for 6 people |

## What to Say

Purchase large fish and small shellfish by weight.

| | |
|---|---|
| 1/2 kilo of … | **Un demi-kilo de…**<br>an der·mee·kee·loh der |
| 1 kilo of … | **Un kilo de…**<br>an kee·loh der |
| 1 1/2 kilos of … | **Un kilo et demi de…**<br>an kee·loh eh der·mee der |
| … cod. | **morue.**<br>moh·roo |
| … mussels. | **moules.**<br>mool |
| … prawns. | **crevettes roses.**<br>crer·vet rohz |
| … red mullet. | **rougets.**<br>roo·sheh |
| … sardines. | **sardines.**<br>sar·deen |

| | |
|---|---|
| ½ kilo of … | **Un demi-kilo de…** |
| | an der·mee·kee·loh der |
| 1 kilo of … | **Un kilo de…** |
| | an kee·loh der |
| 1½ kilos of … | **Un kilo et demi de…** |
| | an kee·loh eh der·mee der |
| … shrimp. | **crevettes grises.** |
| | crer·vet greez |
| … turbot. | **turbot.** |
| | toor·boh |
| … whiting. | **merlans.** |
| | mair·lahn |
| 1 kilo … | **Un kilo…** |
| | an kee·loh |
| … of anchovies. | **d'anchois.** |
| | dahn·shwah |
| … of eel. | **d'anguille.** |
| | dahn·gwee |
| … of oysters. | **d'huîtres.** |
| | dweet |

Some large fish can be purchased by the slice.

| | |
|---|---|
| One slice of … | **Une tranche de…** |
| | oon trahnsh der |
| Two slices of … | **Deux tranches de…** |
| | der trahnsh der |
| Six slices of … | **Six tranches de…** |
| | see tranhsh der |
| … cod. | **cabillaud.** |
| | cah·bee·yoh |
| … salmon. | **saumon.** |
| | soh·mohn |
| … fresh tuna. | **thon.** |
| | tohn |

For some shellfish and "frying pan" fish, specify the number you want.

| | |
|---|---|
| A crab, please. | **Un crabe, s'il vous plaît.** |
| | an crahb sil voo pleh |
| A herring. | **Un hareng.** |
| | an ah·rahn |
| A lobster. | **Une langouste/Un homard.** |
| | oon lahn·goost/an oh·mar |
| A mackerel. | **Un maquereau.** |
| | an mahk·roh |

| | |
|---|---|
| A scallop. | **Une coquille de Saint-Jacques.**<br>oon coh·kee der san shahk |
| A sole. | **Une sole.**<br>oon sohl |
| A trout. | **Une truite.**<br>oon trweet |
| A whiting. | **Un merlan.**<br>an mair·lahn |

For other essential expressions, see "Shop Talk," p. 44.

| | |
|---|---|
| Please can you … | **S'il vous plaît, pouvez-vous…**<br>sil voo pleh poo·veh·voo |
| … take the heads off? | **enlever les têtes?**<br>ahn·ler·veh leh tet |
| … clean them? | **les vider?**<br>leh vee·deh |
| … fillet them? | **les découper en filets?**<br>leh deh·coo·peh ahn fee·leh |

# Eating and Drinking Out

## Ordering a Drink

### Essential Information

- Here are the places to ask for (see p. 10).

  **Bar**
  **Café**

- The price list of drinks (**tarifs de consommations**) must, by law, be displayed outside or in the window.

- There is waiter service in all cafés and bars, but you can drink at the bar or counter if you wish, which is cheaper.

- Always leave a tip of 10% or 15% of the bill unless you see **service compris** or **prix nets** (tip included) printed on the bill or on a notice.

- Bars and cafés serve both alcoholic and non-alcoholic drinks. There are no licensing laws, and children are allowed in.

### What to Say

| | |
|---|---|
| I'd like …, please. | **Je voudrais…, s'il vous plaît.** sher voo·dreh… sil voo pleh |
| … black coffee … | **un café nature/un café noir** an cah·feh nah·toor/an cah·feh nwah |
| … coffee with cream … | **un café crème** an cah·feh crem |
| … hot chocolate … | **un chocolat chaud** an shoh·coh·lah shoh |
| … tea … | **un thé** an teh |
| … with milk … | **au lait** oh leh |
| … with lemon … | **au citron** oh see·trohn |
| … Coca-Cola … | **un Coca-cola** an coh·cah·coh·lah |
| … a glass of milk … | **un verre de lait** an vair der leh |
| … lemonade … | **une limonade** oon lee·moh·nahd |

| | |
|---|---|
| I'd like ..., please. | **Je voudrais…, s'il vous plaît.**<br>sher voo·dreh… sil voo pleh |
| … mineral water … | **un Perrier**<br>an pair·yeh |
| … orangeade … | **une orangeade**<br>oon oh·rahn·shahd |
| … orange juice … | **un jus d'orange**<br>an shoo doh·rahnsh |
| … grape juice … | **un jus de raisin**<br>an shoo der reh·zan |
| … pineapple juice … | **un jus d'ananas**<br>an shoo dah·nah·nah |
| … a beer … | **une bière**<br>oon bee·air |
| … a draft beer … | **une bière pression**<br>oon bee·air pres·syohn |
| … a light ale … | **une Kanterbrau**<br>oon kahn·ter·broh |
| … a lager … | **une Pils**<br>oon pils |
| … a half-pint … | **un demi**<br>an der·mee |
| A glass of … | **Un verre de…**<br>an vair der |
| … red wine. | **vin rouge.**<br>van roosh |
| … white wine. | **vin blanc.**<br>van blahn |
| … rosé wine … | **vin rosé**<br>van roh·zeh |
| … dry. | **sec.**<br>sek |
| … sweet. | **doux.**<br>doo |
| … sparkling wine. | **vin mousseux.**<br>van mooss·er |
| … champagne. | **champagne.**<br>shahm·pahn |
| A whisky … | **Un whisky…**<br>an wees·kee |
| … with ice. | **avec des glaçons.**<br>ah·vek deh glah·sohn |

A whisky …
**Un whisky…**
an wees·kee

… with water.
**à l'eau.**
ah loh

… with soda.
**avec soda.**
ah·vek soh·dah

A gin …
**Un gin…**
an sheen

… and tonic.
**avec Schweppes.**
ah·vek shwep

… with lemon.
**avec citron.**
ah·vek see·trohn

A brandy/cognac.
**Un cognac.**
an coh·nyahk

Here are some local drinks you may like to try.

an apple brandy
**un Calvados**
an cahl·vah·dohs

a freshly squeezed lemon drink
**un citron pressé**
an see·trohn press·eh

an orange liqueur
**un Cointreau**
an cwen·troh

a lemonade and mint cordial
**un diabolo-menthe**
an dee·ah·boh·loh·mahnt

a type of brandy
**une eau de vie**
oon oh der vee

an herb tea (drunk after meals)
**une infusion**
oon an·foo·zyohn

a sweet red wine (aperitif)
**un muscat**
an mooss·caht

a drink made from aniseed
  and brandy (aperitif)
**un Cazanis/un Ricard/
un Pernod/un pastis**
an cah·zah·neess/an ree·car/
an pair·noh/an pahss·teess

Some other essential expressions are the following.

Miss! [*This does not sound
  abrupt in French.*]
**Mademoiselle!**
mahd·mwah·zel

Waiter!
**Garçon!**
gar·sohn

The check, please.
**L'addition, s'il vous plaît.**
lah·dee·syohn sil voo pleh

How much does that come to?
**Ça fait combien?**
sah feh com·bee·an

| | |
|---|---|
| Is the tip included? | **Est-ce que le service est compris?**<br>es ker ler sair·veess eh com·pree |
| Where are the restrooms, please? | **Où sont les WC, s'il vous plaît?**<br>oo sohn leh veh·seh sil voo pleh |

# Ordering a Snack

## Essential Information

· Look for cafés or bars with the following signs.

**Casse-croûte à toute heure**      Snacks at any time
**Sandwichs**

· You will find the names of snacks on signs in the window or on side-walk signs.

· In some regions, mobile vans sell hot snacks.

· For cakes, see p. 49. For ice cream, see p. 51. For picnic food, see p. 55.

## What to Say

| | |
|---|---|
| I'd like …, please. | **Je voudrais…, s'il vous plaît.**<br>sher voo·dreh… sil voo pleh |
| … a cheese sandwich … | **un sandwich au fromage**<br>an sahnd·wich oh froh·mahsh |
| … a ham sandwich … | **un sandwich au jambon**<br>an sahnd·wich oh shahm·bohn |
| … a crepe … | **une crêpe**<br>oon crep |

Here are some other snacks you might like to try.

| | |
|---|---|
| sauerkraut served with ham and sausage | **une choucroute garnie**<br>oon shoo·croot gar·nee |
| toasted ham and cheese sandwich | **un croque-monsieur**<br>an crok·mer·syer |
| chips | **des frites**<br>deh freet |
| a hot dog | **un hot-dog**<br>an oht·dog |
| a salami sandwich | **un sandwich au saucisson**<br>an sahnd·wich oh soh·see·sohn |
| a pâté sandwich | **un sandwich au pâté**<br>an sahnd·wich oh pah·teh |

For other essential expressions, see "Ordering a Drink," p. 67.

# In a Restaurant

## Essential Information

- The place to look for is **un restaurant** (see p. 11).
- You can eat at any of the following places.

| | |
|---|---|
| **Restaurant** | |
| **Café** | |
| **Buffet** | At stations |
| **Routiers** | Truck stops |
| **Brasserie** | Informal restaurant with simple but hearty fare |
| **Relais** | |
| **Auberge** | |
| **Rôtisserie** | |
| **Drugstore** | |
| **Bistro** | |
| **Libre-service** | Self-service cafeterias on the outskirts of towns or in superstores |

- By law, menus must be displayed outside or in the window. This is a helpful way to judge if a place suits you before entering.
- Self-service restaurants are not unknown, but all other places have waiter service.
- You should leave a tip unless you see **service compris** on the bill or on the menu.
- Children's portions are not usually available.
- Eating times are usually from noon to 2:30 P.M. and from 7:00 P.M. to 11:00 P.M., but these vary a great deal according to the type of establishment.

## What to Say

| | |
|---|---|
| May I reserve a table? | **Puis-je réserver une table?** pweesh reh·zair·veh oon tahb |
| I have reserved a table. | **J'ai réservé une table.** sheh reh·zair·veh oon tahb |
| A table … | **Une table…** oon tahb |
| … for one. | **pour une personne.** poor oon pair·son |
| … for three. | **pour trois personnes.** poor trwah pair·son |

| | |
|---|---|
| The à la carte menu, please. | **La carte, s'il vous plaît.**<br>la cart sil voo pleh |
| The fixed price menu. | **Le menu à prix fixe.**<br>ler mer·noo ah pree feex |
| The tourist menu. | **Le menu touristique.**<br>ler mer·noo toor·ee·steek |
| Today's special menu. | **Le menu du jour.**<br>ler mer·noo doo shoor |
| The wine list. | **La carte des vins.**<br>lah cart deh van |
| What's this, please? [*point to an item on the menu*] | **Qu'est ce que c'est ça, s'il vous plaît?**<br>kes ker seh sah sil voo pleh |
| A carafe of wine, please. | **Une carafe de vin, s'il vous plaît.**<br>oon car·ahf der van sil voo pleh |
| A quarter (liter) (250 cc). | **Un quart.**<br>an car |
| A half (liter) (500 cc). | **Une demi-carafe.**<br>oon der·mee·cah·rahf |
| A glass. | **Un verre.**<br>an vair |
| A bottle./A liter. | **Une bouteille./Un litre.**<br>oon boo·tay/an leet |
| A half-bottle. | **Une demi-bouteille.**<br>oon der·mee·boo·tay |
| Red/white/rosé/house wine. | **Du vin rouge/blanc/rosé/maison.**<br>doo van roosh/blahn/roh·zeh/<br>meh·zohn |
| Some more bread, please. | **Encore du pain, s'il vous plaît.**<br>ahn·cor doo pan sil voo pleh |
| Some more wine. | **Encore du vin.**<br>ahn·cor doo van |
| Some oil. | **De l'huile.**<br>der lweel |
| Some vinegar. | **Du vinaigre.**<br>doo vee·neg |
| Some salt. | **Du sel.**<br>doo sel |
| Some pepper. | **Du poivre.**<br>doo pwahv |
| Some water. | **De l'eau.**<br>der loh |
| With/without (garlic). | **Sans/avec de (l'ail).**<br>sahn/ah·vek der (lye) |

| | |
|---|---|
| Miss! [*This does not sound abrupt in French.*] | **Mademoiselle!**<br>mahd·mwah·zel |
| Waiter! | **Garçon!**<br>gar·sohn |
| The check, please. | **L'addition, s'il vous plaît.**<br>lah·dee·syohn sil voo pleh |
| How much does that come to? | **Ça fait combien?**<br>sah feh com·bee·an |
| Is the tip included? | **Est-ce que le service est compris?**<br>es ker ler sair·veess eh com·pree |
| Where are the restrooms, please? | **Où sont les WC, s'il vous plaît?**<br>oon sohn leh veh·seh sil voo pleh |

Here are some key words for meal courses, as seen on many menus.

| | |
|---|---|
| What have you got in the way of … | **Qu'est-ce que vous avez comme…**<br>kes ker voo·zah·veh com |
| … appetizers? | **hors d'œuvre?**<br>or derv |
| … soup? | **soupe?**<br>soop |
| … egg dishes? | **œufs?**<br>erf |
| … fish? | **poisson?**<br>pwah·sohn |
| … meat? | **viande?**<br>vee·ahnd |
| … game? | **gibier?**<br>sheeb·yeh |
| … fowl? | **volaille?**<br>voh·lye |
| … vegetables? | **légumes?**<br>leh·goom |
| … cheese? | **fromages?**<br>froh·mahsh |
| … ice cream? | **glaces?**<br>glahss |
| … dessert? | **dessert?**<br>deh·sair |

# Understanding the Menu

- The main ingredients of most dishes are given on the following pages.

Together with the following list of cooking and menu terms, the ingredient lists should help you decode a menu.

- These cooking and menu terms are for understanding only; for this reason, no pronunciation guide is given.

## Cooking and Menu Terms

| | |
|---|---|
| **à l'anglaise** | boiled |
| **au beurre** | with butter |
| **au beurre noir** | fried in sizzling butter |
| **bien cuit** | well done |
| **bisque** | shellfish soup |
| **blanquette** | cooked in a creamy sauce |
| **au bleu** | boiled in water, oil, and thyme (fish); very rare (meat) |
| **bonne femme** | baked with wine and vegetables |
| **bouilli** | boiled |
| **braisé** | braised |
| **en broche** | spit-roasted |
| **en cocotte** | stewed |
| **coquille** | cooked in a white sauce and browned under the grill |
| **en croûte** | in a pastry shell |
| **en daube** | braised in a wine stock |
| **à l'étouffée** | stewed |
| **farci** | stuffed |
| **au four** | baked |
| **à la française** | cooked with lettuce and onion |
| **frit** | fried |
| **froid** | cold |

| | |
|---|---|
| **fumé** | smoked |
| **garni** | served with vegetables or chips |
| **au gratin** | sprinkled with breadcrumbs and browned |
| **grillé** | grilled |
| **haché** | minced |
| **maître d'hôtel** | served with butter mixed with parsley and lemon juice |
| **Marengo** | cooked in oil, tomatoes, and white wine |
| **mousseline** | mousse |
| **Parmentier** | containing potatoes |
| **poché** | poached |
| **à point** | medium |
| **à la provençale** | cooked with garlic, tomatoes, olive oil, olives, onions, and herbs |
| **rôti** | roasted |
| **saignant** | rare |
| **salade** | served with oil and vinegar |
| **sauce béarnaise** | vinegar, egg yolks, white wine, butter, shallots, and tarragon |
| **sauce béchamel** | flour, butter, and milk |
| **sauce bourguignonne** | red wine sauce with herbs, onions, and spices |
| **sauce madère** | cooked in Madeira wine |
| **sauce Mornay** | cheese sauce |
| **sauce piquante** | sharp vinegar sauce with chopped gherkins and herbs |
| **sauté** | fried slowly in butter |
| **en terrine** | preparation of meat, game, or fowl baked in a terrine (casserole) and served cold |
| **à la vapeur** | steamed |
| **Vichy** | garnished with carrots |
| **vinaigrette** | with oil and vinegar |

## Ingredients and Other Helpful Menu Terms

| | |
|---|---|
| **assiette anglaise** | cold meat and salad |
| **boudin** | black pudding |
| **bouillabaisse** | rich fish soup featuring a variety of fish and shellfish |
| **champignons** | mushrooms |
| **chantilly** | cream whipped with icing sugar |

| | |
|---|---|
| **choucroute** | sauerkraut |
| **compote** | stewed fruit |
| **consommé** | clear broth |
| **crudités** | raw vegetables served as appetizers |
| **cuisses de grenouilles** | frogs' legs |
| **escalopes panées** | veal chops fried in egg and breadcrumbs |
| **escargots** | snails |
| **flan** | egg custard |
| **moules** | mussels |
| **potage** | vegetable soup |
| **quenelles** | fish or meat fingers cooked in a white sauce |
| **ragoût** | stew |
| **ratatouille** | a vegetable stew |
| **ris de veau** | veal sweetbreads |
| **sorbet** | sorbet |
| **tournedos** | fillet steak |

# Health

## Essential Information

- For details of reciprocal health agreements between your country and France, visit your local Department of Health office at least one month before leaving, or ask your travel agent.

- It is a good idea to purchase a medical insurance policy through a travel agent, an insurance broker, or a travel organization.

- Take an "emergency" first-aid kit with you.

- For minor health problems and treatment at a drugstore, see p. 31.

- For asking the way to a doctor, dentist, drugstore, or Social Security Office, see p. 12.

- Once in France, determine a plan of action in case of serious illness: communicate your problem to a neighbor, the receptionist, or someone you see regularly. You are then dependent on that person to help you obtain treatment.

- To find a doctor in an emergency, look for **Médecins** in the Yellow Pages of the telephone directory. Here are important signs to look for.

| | |
|---|---|
| **Urgences** | Emergency room |
| **H** | Hospital |
| **Hôpital** | Hospital |

## What's the Matter?

| | |
|---|---|
| I have a pain … | **J'ai mal…**<br>sheh mahl |
| … in my abdomen. | **au ventre.**<br>oh vahnt |
| … in my ankle. | **à la cheville.**<br>ah lah sher·vee |
| … in my arm. | **au bras.**<br>oh brah |
| … in my back. | **au dos.**<br>oh doh |
| … in my bladder. | **à la vessie.**<br>ah lah veh·see |
| … in my bowels. | **à l'intestin.**<br>ah lan·teh·stan |
| … in my breast. | **au sein.**<br>oh san |

| | |
|---|---|
| I have a pain … | **J'ai mal…**<br>sheh mahl |
| … in my chest. | **à la poitrine.**<br>ah lah pwah·treen |
| … in my ear. | **à l'oreille.**<br>ah loh·ray |
| … in my eye. | **à l'œil.**<br>ah ler |
| … in my foot. | **au pied.**<br>oh pee·eh |
| … in my head. | **à la tête.**<br>ah lah tet |
| … in my heel. | **au talon.**<br>oh tah·lohn |
| … in my jaw. | **à la mâchoire.**<br>ah lah mah·shwah |
| … in my kidney. | **au rein.**<br>oh ran |
| … in my leg. | **à la jambe.**<br>ah lah shahmb |
| … in my lung. | **au poumon.**<br>oh poo·mohn |
| … in my neck. | **au cou.**<br>oh coo |
| … in my penis. | **au pénis.**<br>oh peh·neess |
| … in my shoulder. | **à l'épaule.**<br>ah leh·pohl |
| … in my stomach. | **à l'estomac.**<br>ah leh·stoh·mah |
| … in my testicle. | **au testicule.**<br>oh teh·stee·cool |
| … in my throat. | **à la gorge.**<br>ah lah gorsh |
| … in my vagina. | **au vagin.**<br>oh vah·shan |
| … in my wrist. | **au poignet.**<br>oh pwah·nyeh |
| I have a pain here. [*point*] | **J'ai mal ici.**<br>sheh mahl ee·see |
| I have a toothache. | **J'ai mal aux dents.**<br>sheh mahl oh dahn |

| | |
|---|---|
| I have broken … | **J'ai cassé…**<br>sheh cah·seh |
| … my dentures. | **mon dentier.**<br>mohn dahn·tyeh |
| … my glasses. | **mes lunettes.**<br>meh loo·net |
| I have lost … | **J'ai perdu…**<br>sheh pair·doo |
| … my contact lenses. | **mes verres de contact.**<br>meh vair der cohn·tahkt |
| … a filling. | **un plombage.**<br>an plohm·bahsh |
| My child is ill. | **Mon enfant est malade.**<br>moh·nahn·fahn eh mah·lahd |
| He/she has a pain in his/her … | **Il** (*male*)/**Elle** (*female*) **a mal…**<br>il/el ah mahl |
| … ankle. [*see list above*] | **à la cheville.**<br>ah lah sher·vee |

## How Bad Is It?

| | |
|---|---|
| I am ill. | **Je suis malade.**<br>sher swee mah·lahd |
| It is urgent. | **C'est urgent.**<br>seh·toor·shahn |
| It is serious. | **C'est grave.**<br>seh grahv |
| It is not serious. | **Ce n'est pas grave.**<br>ser neh pah grahv |
| It hurts. | **Ça me fait mal.**<br>sah mer feh mahl |
| It hurts a lot. | **Ça me fait très mal.**<br>sah mer feh treh mahl |
| It does not hurt much. | **Ça ne me fait pas très mal.**<br>sah ner mer feh pah treh mahl |
| The pain occurs … | **La douleur revient…**<br>lah doo·ler rer·vee·an |
| … every quarter of an hour. | **tous les quarts d'heure.**<br>too leh car der |
| … every half hour. | **toutes les demi-heures.**<br>toot leh der·mee·er |
| … every hour. | **toutes les heures.**<br>toot leh·zer |
| … every day. | **tous les jours.**<br>too leh shoor |

| | |
|---|---|
| It hurts most of the time. | **C'est une douleur continue.**<br>seh·toon doo·ler cohn·tee·noo |
| I have had it for ... | **Ça me fait mal depuis...**<br>sah mer feh mahl der·pwee |
| ... one hour/one day. | **une heure/un jour.**<br>oon er/an shoor |
| ... two hours/two days. | **deux heures/deux jours.**<br>der·zer/der shoor |
| It is a ... | **C'est une...**<br>seh·toon |
| ... sharp pain. | **douleur aiguë.**<br>doo·ler eg·goo |
| ... dull ache. | **douleur sourde.**<br>doo·ler soord |
| ... nagging pain. | **douleur irritante.**<br>doo·ler eer·ree·tahnt |
| I feel ... | **J'ai...**<br>sheh |
| ... dizzy. | **des vertiges.**<br>deh vair·teesh |
| ... sick. | **la nausée.**<br>lah noh·zeh |
| I feel ... | **Je me sens...**<br>sher mer sahn |
| ... feverish. | **fiévreux** (*male*)/**fiévreuse** (*female*).<br>fee·ev·rer/fee·ev·rerz |
| ... weak. | **faible.**<br>feb |

Are you already being treated for something else?

| | |
|---|---|
| I take ... regularly. [*show medication*] | **Je prends... régulièrement.**<br>sher prahn... reh·goo·lyair·mahn |
| ... this medicine ... | **ce médicament**<br>ser meh·dee·cah·mahn |
| ... these pills... | **ces pilules**<br>seh pee·lool |
| I have ... | **J'ai...**<br>sheh |
| ... a heart condition. | **le cœur malade.**<br>ler ker mah·lahd |
| ... hemorrhoids. | **des hémorroïdes.**<br>deh·zeh·moh·roh·eed |

| | |
|---|---|
| I have … | **J'ai…** |
| | sheh |
| … rheumatism. | **des rhumatismes.** |
| | deh roo·mah·teesm |
| I am … | **Je suis…** |
| | sher swee |
| … allergic to (penicillin). | **allergique à (la pénicilline).** |
| | ah·lair·sheek ah |
| | (lah peh·nee·see·leen) |
| … asthmatic. | **asthmatique.** |
| | ahs·mah·teek |
| … diabetic. | **diabétique.** |
| | dee·ah·beh·teek |
| … pregnant. | **enceinte.** |
| | ahn·sant |

## Other Essential Expressions

| | |
|---|---|
| Please, can you help me? | **Pouvez-vous m'aider, s'il vous plaît?** |
| | pooh·veh·voo meh·deh sil voo pleh |
| A doctor, please. | **Un docteur, s'il vous plaît.** |
| | an doc·ter sil voo pleh |
| A dentist. | **Un dentiste.** |
| | an dahn·teest |
| I don't speak French. | **Je ne parle pas français.** |
| | sher ner parl pah frahn·seh |
| (At) what time does … arrive? | **À quelle heure arrive…** |
| | ah kel er ah·reev |
| … the doctor … | **le docteur?** |
| | ler doc·ter |
| … the dentist … | **le dentiste?** |
| | ler dahn·teest |

Here are important things the doctor may tell you.

| | |
|---|---|
| Take this … | **Prenez ceci…** |
| | prer·neh ser·see |
| … every day. | **tous les jours.** |
| | too leh shoor |
| … every hour. | **toutes les heures.** |
| | toot leh·zer |
| … four times a day. | **quatre fois par jour.** |
| | kat fwah par shoor |

Stay in bed.

**Gardez le lit.**
gar·deh ler lee

Don't travel for _____
days/weeks.

**Ne voyagez pas avant _____
jours/semaines.**
ner vwah·yah·sheh pah·zah·vahn…
shoor/ser·men

You must go to the hospital.

**Vous devez aller à l'hôpital.**
voo der·veh·zah·leh ah loh·pee·tahl

# Problems: Complaints, Loss, and Theft

## Essential Information

- If you have problems with …

    … camping facilities, see p. 25.
    … household appliances, see p. 28.
    … your health, see p. 77.
    … a car, see p. 96.

- If worse comes to worst, find the police station. To ask directions, see p. 9.

- Look for the following signs.

| | |
|---|---|
| **Gendarmerie** | Police |
| **Commissariat de Police** | Police station |

- If you lose your passport, report the loss to the police and go to your nearest Consulate.

- Emergencies: Dial 15 for a medical emergency. This is the number for **SAMU (Services d'aide médicale urgent)**. Dial 17 for the police (**la police**) and 18 for the fire department (**les pompiers**).

## Complaints

| | |
|---|---|
| I bought this … | **J'ai acheté ça…** |
| | sheh ahsh·teh sah |
| … today. | **aujourd'hui.** |
| | oh·shoor·dwee |
| … yesterday. | **hier.** |
| | ee·air |
| … on Monday. | **lundi.** |
| | lern·dee |

For days of the week, see p. 116.

| | |
|---|---|
| It is no good (not suitable). | **Ça ne va pas.** |
| | sah ner vah pah |
| It is defective. | **Il y a un défaut.** |
| | il yah an deh·foh |
| Look. | **Regardez.** |
| | rer·gar·deh |

| | |
|---|---|
| Here. [*point*] | **Ici.**<br>ee·see |
| Can you ... | **Pouvez-vous...**<br>poo·veh·voo |
| ... exchange it? | **l'échanger?**<br>leh·shahn·sheh |
| ... give me a refund? | **me rembourser?**<br>mer rahm·boor·seh |
| ... repair it? | **le réparer?**<br>ler reh·pah·reh |
| Here's the receipt. | **Voici le reçu.**<br>vwah·see ler rer·soo |
| Can I see the manager? | **Puis-je voir le directeur?**<br>pweesh vwah ler dee·rek·ter |

## Loss

See also "Theft" below. The lists are interchangeable.

| | |
|---|---|
| I have lost ... | **J'ai perdu...**<br>sheh pair·doo |
| ... my bag. | **mon sac.**<br>mohn sahk |
| ... my camera. | **mon appareil photo.**<br>mohn ah·pah·ray foh·toh |
| ... my car keys. | **les clés de ma voiture.**<br>leh cleh der mah vwah·toor |
| ... my driver's license. | **mon permis de conduire.**<br>mohn pair·mee der cohn·dweer |
| ... my insurance papers. | **mon assurance.**<br>mohn ah·soo·rahns |
| ... my purse. | **mon sac à main.**<br>mohn sahk ah man |
| I have lost everything! | **J'ai tout perdu!**<br>sheh too pair·doo |

## Theft

See also "Loss" above. The lists are interchangeable.

| | |
|---|---|
| Someone has stolen ... | **On m'a volé...**<br>ohn mah voh·leh |
| ... my bracelet. | **mon bracelet.**<br>mohn brahss·leh |
| ... my car. | **ma voiture.**<br>mah vwah·toor |

| | |
|---|---|
| Someone has stolen … | **On m'a volé…**<br>ohn mah voh·leh |
| … my car radio. | **mon autoradio.**<br>moh·noh·toh·rah·dyoh |
| … my jewelry. | **mes bijoux.**<br>meh bee·shoo |
| … my keys. | **mes clés.**<br>meh cleh |
| … my luggage. | **mes bagages.**<br>meh bah·gahsh |
| … my money. | **mon argent.**<br>moh·nar·shahn |
| … my necklace. | **mon collier.**<br>mohn cohl·yeh |
| … my passport. | **mon passeport.**<br>mohn pahss·por |
| … my radio. | **mon transistor.**<br>mohn trahn·see·stor |
| … my tickets. | **mes billets.**<br>meh bee·yeh |
| … my traveler's checks. | **mes chèques-voyage.**<br>meh shek·vwah·yahsh |
| … my wallet. | **mon portefeuille.**<br>mohn port·fer·ee |
| … my watch. | **ma montre.**<br>mah mohnt |

## Likely Reactions

| | |
|---|---|
| Wait. | **Attendez.**<br>ah·tahn·deh |
| When? | **Quand?**<br>kahn |
| Where? | **Où?**<br>oo |
| Your name? | **Nom?**<br>nohm |
| Address? | **Adresse?**<br>ah·dress |
| I can't help you. | **Je ne puis rien pour vous.**<br>sher ner pwee ree·an poor voo |
| I can't do anything about it. | **Ce n'est pas ici qu'il faut s'adresser.**<br>ser neh pah·zee·see keel foh sah·dreh·seh |

# The Post Office

### Essential Information

- For finding a post office, see p. 9.

- Here are signs to look for.

    **La Poste**
    **Postes**
    **Poste, Télégraphe, Téléphone (PTT)**
    **Postes et Télécommunications (PT)**

- Look for the sign below.

    # LA POSTE ➤

- It is best to buy stamps at a to-bacco shop (**le tabac**). Go to the post office (**la poste**) only for more complicated transactions, such as mailing a package. Look for the signs at right.

- Letter boxes in France are yellow (in Belgium, red).

- To have your mail held through general delivery (**poste restante**), you will need to show your passport at the counter marked **Poste Restante** in the main post office; you will pay a small charge.

### What to Say

| | |
|---|---|
| To the United States, please.<br>[*hand letters, cards, or packages over the counter*] | **Pour les États-Unis, s'il vous plaît.**<br>poor leh·zeh·tah·zoo·nee sil voo pleh |
| To Australia. | **Pour l'Australie.**<br>poor loh·strah·lee |
| To Canada. | **Pour le Canada.**<br>poor ler cah·nah·dah |

For names of other countries, see p. 120.

| | |
|---|---|
| How much is … | **C'est combien…**<br>seh com·bee·an |
| … this package (to the United States)? | **ce colis (pour les États-Unis)?**<br>ser coh·lee (poor leh·zeh·tah·zoo·nee) |
| … a letter (to Canada)? | **une lettre (pour le Canada)?**<br>oon let (poor ler cah·nah·dah) |
| … a postcard (to Australia)? | **une carte postale (pour l'Australie)?**<br>oon cart poh·stahl (poor loh·strah·lee) |
| Air mail. | **Par avion.**<br>par ah·vyohn |
| Surface mail. | **Ordinaire.**<br>or·dee·nair |
| One stamp, please. | **Un timbre, s'il vous plaît.**<br>an tamb sil voo pleh |
| Two stamps. | **Deux timbres.**<br>der tamb |
| One (one-euro) stamp. | **Un timbre (un euro).**<br>an tamb (an er·oh) |
| One (15-centime) stamp. | **Un timbre (quinze centimes).**<br>an tamb (kanz sahn·teem) |
| I would like to send a telegram. | **Je voudrais envoyer une télégramme.**<br>sher voo·dreh·zahn·vwah·yeh oon teh·leh·grahm |

# Telephoning

## Essential Information

- Unless you read and speak French well, it is best not to make phone calls by yourself. You should go to the main post office and write the town and number you want on a piece of paper. Add **avec préavis** if you want a person-to-person call or **PCV** if you want to reverse the charges.

- Public telephones are located in most public places: in post offices, railway stations, metro stations, and shopping arcades, as well as in kiosks on the street.

- Most public telephones are card-operated. **Télécartes** are available at tobacco shops, post offices, newspaper kiosks, and France Télécom stores. Each card has either 50 or 120 units.

- To make a call from a public telephone, insert the **télécarte** or put the appropriate coins in the slot, then lift the receiver and wait for the dial tone. Dial the telephone number you want to reach. If you are using cash, you will need to put in additional coins when the **Épuisé** sign lights up.

- You may wish to consider renting or purchasing a pre-pay European cell phone while in France.

- For international calls, it is easier to use newer phones that take international calling cards, which are available at tobacco shops. If you use an international calling card, dial the access number on the back of the card. You will be prompted to dial the PIN number for the card, then the number you want to reach.

- Alternatively, dial the appropriate access number for AT&T, MCI, or Sprint, and you can have the charges applied to a credit card.

- To call the United States, dial country code 1, then the area code and number you want to call. Canada's country code is also 1.

- To ask the way to a public telephone, see p. 12.

## What to Say

| | |
|---|---|
| Where can I make a telephone call? | **Où puis-je téléphoner?**<br>oo pweesh teh·leh·foh·neh |
| Local/long distance. | **Dans la région/à l'étranger.**<br>dahn lah reh·shyohn/<br>ah leh·trahn·sheh |
| I'd like this number ... [*show number*] | **Je voudrais ce numéro…**<br>sher voo·dreh ser noo·meh·roh |
| … in the United States. | **aux États-Unis.**<br>oh·zeh·tah·zoo·nee |
| … in Australia. | **en Australie.**<br>ahn oh·strah·lee |
| … in Canada. | **au Canada.**<br>oh cah·nah·dah |

For names of other countries, see p. 120.

| | |
|---|---|
| Can you dial it for me, please? | **Pouvez-vous me l'appeler, s'il vous plaît?**<br>poo·veh·voo mer lahp·leh sil voo pleh |
| How much is it? | **C'est combien?**<br>seh com·bee·an |
| Hello! | **Allô!**<br>ahl·loh |
| May I speak to _____? | **Puis-je parler à _____?**<br>pweesh par·leh ah… |
| Extension _____. | **Poste _____.**<br>pohst… |
| I'm sorry, I don't speak French. | **Je regrette, je ne parle pas français.**<br>sher rer·gret sher ner parl pah frahn·seh |
| Do you speak English? | **Parlez-vous anglais?**<br>par·leh·voo·zahn·gleh |
| Thank you. I'll call back. | **Merci. Je rappellerai.**<br>mair·see sher rah·pel·reh |
| Good-bye. | **Au revoir.**<br>oh rer·vwah |

## Likely Reactions

| | |
|---|---|
| That's 80 cents. | **C'est huitante cents d'euros.**<br>seh wee·tahnt sahn der·roh |

Booth number (3).

**Cabine numéro (trois).**
cah·been noo·meh·roh (trwah)

For numbers, see p. 112.

For numbers, see p. 112.

Don't hang up.

**Ne quittez pas.**
ner kee·teh pah

I am trying to connect you.

**J'essaie de vous passer l'abonné.**
sheh·seh der voo pah·seh
lah·boh·neh

Go ahead; you're connected.

**Parlez.**
par·leh

There's a delay.

**Il y a une attente.**
il yah oon at·tahnt

I'll try again.

**J'essaie encore (une fois).**
sheh·seh ahn·cor (oon fwah)

# Cashing Checks and Changing Money

## Essential Information

- To ask directions to a bank or currency exchange office, see p. 10.
- Look for the following words to find places for banking.

  **Banque**               **Bureau de Change**
  **Crédit**               **Change**
  **Société Générale**

- You may access funds from your United States bank at most ATMs by using your ATM card. The machine should have instructions in a number of languages, including English. Look for one of the following signs.

  **Guichet Automatique de Banque**
  **GAB**
  **Guichet Automatique**
  **GA**
  **Guichet Bancaire**
  **Automate Bancaire**

- Be sure to have your passport handy.

## What to Say

| | |
|---|---|
| I'd like to cash … | **Je voudrais encaisser…**<br>sher voo·dreh ahn·keh·seh |
| … this traveler's check. | **ce chèque-voyage.**<br>ser shek·vwah·yahsh |
| … these traveler's checks. | **ces chèques-voyage.**<br>seh shek·vwah·yahsh |
| I'd like to change this into euros. | **Je voudrais changer ceci en euros.**<br>sher voo·dreh shahn·sheh ser·see ahn er·roh |
| Here is … | **Voici…**<br>vwah·see |
| … my ATM card. | **ma carte.**<br>mah cart |
| … my passport. | **mon passeport.**<br>mohn pahss·por |
| What is the exchange rate? | **Quel est le taux de change?**<br>kel eh ler toh der shahnsh |

## Likely Reactions

| | |
|---|---|
| Passport, please. | **Passeport, s'il vous plaît.**<br>pahss·por sil voo pleh |
| Sign here. | **Signez ici.**<br>see·nyeh ee·see |
| Your ATM card, please. | **Votre carte, s'il vous plaît.**<br>voht cart sil voo pleh |
| Go to the cashier's window. | **Passez à la caisse.**<br>pah·seh ah lah kess |

# Automobile Travel

## Essential Information

- To ask directions to a gas station or garage, see p. 11.
- If you would like to find a gas station, look for the following signs.

  **Station-service**       **Poste d'essence**
  **Station libre-service**  **Carburant**
  **Essence**

- There are three grades of gasoline.

  **Ordinaire**   Standard
  **Super**       Premium
  **Gazole**      Diesel

- One gallon is about 3¾ liters (accurate enough up to 6 gallons).
- For car repairs, look for the following signs.

  **Dépannage**   Repairs      **Mécanicien**   Mechanic
  **Garage**      Garage       **Carrosserie**  Body work

- Gas stations on major highways (**autoroutes**) are always open. However, in small towns and on side roads, stations may close in the middle of the day, between noon and 3:00 P.M.
- Roadside assistance: If you are driving a rental car in France, roadside assistance for a breakdown or emergency is typically linked to your car rental program; consult the informational material from your car rental agency.
- For road signs and warnings, see p. 108.

## What to Say

For numbers, see p. 112.

| | |
|---|---|
| (Nine) liters … | **(Neuf) litres...** |
| | (nerf) leet |
| (Thirty) euros' worth … | **(Trente) euros...** |
| | trahnt er·roh |
| … of standard. | **d'ordinaire.** |
| | dor·dee·nair |
| … of premium. | **de super.** |
| | der soo·pair |
| … of diesel. | **de gazole.** |
| | der gah·zohl |

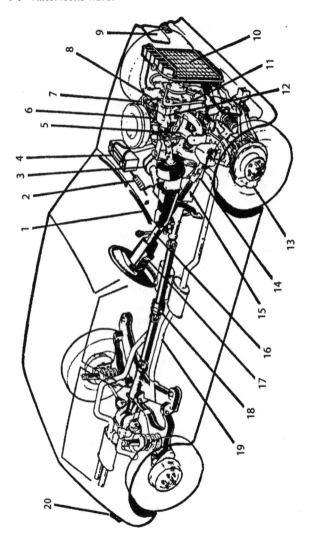

| | | | |
|---|---|---|---|
| 1 | windshield wipers | **essuie-glace** eh-swee-glahss | |
| 2 | fuses | **fusibles** foo-zeeb | |
| 3 | heater | **chauffage** shoh-fahsh | |
| 4 | battery | **batterie** bah-tree | |
| 5 | engine | **moteur** moh-ter | |
| 6 | fuel pump | **pompe à essence** pomp ah eh-sahns | |
| 7 | starter | **démarreur** deh-mah-rer | |
| 8 | carburetor | **carburateur** car-boo-rah-ter | |
| 9 | headlights | **phares** far | |
| 10 | radiator | **radiateur** rah-dee-ah-ter | |

| | | |
|---|---|---|
| 11 | fan belt | **courroie de ventilation** coo-rwah der vahn-tee-lah-syohn |
| 12 | generator | **générateur** sheh-neh-rah-ter |
| 13 | brakes | **freins** fran |
| 14 | clutch | **embrayage** ahm-breh-yahsh |
| 15 | gear box | **boîte à vitesses** bwaht ah vee-tess |
| 16 | steering | **direction** dee-rek-syohn |
| 17 | ignition | **allumage** ah-loo-mahsh |
| 18 | transmission | **transmission** trahns-mee-syohn |
| 19 | exhaust pipe | **tuyau d'échappement** twee-yoh deh-shahp-mahn |
| 20 | turn signals | **clignotants** clee-nyoh-tahn |

Fill it up, please. **Faites le plein, s'il vous plaît.**
fet ler plan sil voo pleh

Will you check … **Pouvez-vous vérifier…**
poo·veh·voo veh·ree·fyeh

… the battery? **la batterie?**
lah bah·tree

… the oil? **l'huile?**
lweel

… the radiator? **le radiateur?**
ler rah·dee·ah·ter

… the tires? **les pneus?**
leh pner

I have run out of gasoline. **Je suis en panne d'essence.**
sher swee·zahn pahn deh·sahns

Can I borrow a can, please? **Puis-je emprunter un bidon,
s'il vous plaît?**
pweesh ahm·prern·teh an
bee·dohn sil voo pleh

My car has broken down. **Ma voiture est en panne.**
mah vwah·toor eh ahn pahn

My car won't start. **Ma voiture ne démarre pas.**
mah vwah·toor ner deh·mar pah

I have had an accident. **J'ai eu un accident.**
sheh er an ahk·see·dahn

I have lost my car keys. **J'ai perdu les clés de ma voiture.**
sheh pair·doo leh cleh der mah
vwah·toor

My car is … **Ma voiture est…**
mah vwah·toor eh

… two kilometers away. **à deux kilomètres.**
ah der kee·loh·met

… three kilometers away. **à trois kilomètres.**
ah trwah kee·loh·met

Can you help me, please? **Pouvez-vous m'aider, s'il vous
plaît?**
poo·veh·voo meh·deh sil voo pleh

Do you repair cars? **Est-ce que vous faites les
réparations?**
es ker voo fet leh reh·pah·rah·syohn

I have a flat tire. **J'ai un pneu à plat.**
sheh an pner ah plaht

I have a broken windshield. **Mon pare-brise est cassé.**
mohn par·breez eh cah·seh

| | |
|---|---|
| I think the problem is here. [*point*] | **Je crois que c'est ça qui ne va pas.** sher crwah ker seh sah kee ner vah pah |
| I don't know what's wrong. | **Je ne sais pas ce qui ne va pas.** sher ner seh pah ser kee ner vah pah |
| Can you … | **Pouvez-vous…** poo·veh·voo |
| … repair it? | **faire la réparation?** fair lah reh·pah·rah·syohn |
| … come and look? | **venir voir?** ver·neer vwah |
| … give me an estimate? | **me donner un prix?** mer doh·neh an pree |
| … write it down? | **l'écrire?** leh·creer |
| How long will it take to repair it? | **Combien de temps prendra la réparation?** com·bee·an der tahn prahn·drah lah reh·pah·rah·syohn |
| When will the car be ready? | **La voiture sera prête quand?** lah vwah·toor ser·rah pret kahn |
| Can I see the bill? | **Puis-je voir la note?** pweesh vwah lah noht |
| This is my insurance information. | **Voici mon assurance.** vwah·see moh·nah·soo·rahns |

## Renting a Car

| | |
|---|---|
| Can I rent a car? | **Puis-je louer une voiture?** pweesh loo·eh oon vwah·toor |
| I need a car … | **J'ai besoin d'une voiture…** sheh ber·zwan doon vwah·toor |
| … for two people … | **pour deux personnes** poor der pair·son |
| … for five people … | **pour cinq personnes** poor sank pair·son |
| … for one day. | **pour une journée.** poor oon shoor·neh |
| … for five days. | **pour cinq jours.** poor sank shoor |
| … for a week. | **pour une semaine.** poor oon ser·men |

Can you write down …

**Pouvez-vous écrire…**
poo·veh·voo eh·creer

… the deposit to pay?

**les arrhes à verser?**
leh·zar ah vair·seh

… the charge per kilometer?

**le tarif au kilomètre?**
ler tah·reef oh kee·loh·met

… the daily charge?

**le tarif à la journée?**
ler tah·reef ah lah shoor·neh

… the cost of insurance?

**le montant de l'assurance?**
ler mohn·tahn der lah·soo·rahns

Can I leave it in (Paris)?

**Puis-je la laisser à (Paris)?**
pweesh lah leh·seh ah (pah·ree)

What documents do I need?

**Quels papiers me faut-il?**
kel pah·pyeh mer foh·teel

## Likely Reactions

I don't do repairs.

**Je ne fais pas les réparations.**
sher ner feh pah leh
reh·pah·rah·syohn

Where is your car?

**Où est votre voiture?**
oo eh voht vwah·toor

What make is it?

**C'est quelle marque?**
seh kel mark

Come back tomorrow/
on Monday.

**Revenez demain/lundi.**
rer·veh·neh der·man/lern·dee

For days of the week, see p. 116.

We don't rent cars.

**On ne fait pas la location.**
on ner feh pah lah loh·cah·syohn

Your driver's license, please.

**Votre permis, s'il vous plaît.**
voht pair·mee sil voo pleh

The mileage is unlimited.

**Le kilométrage n'est pas limité.**
ler kee·loh·meh·trahsh neh pah
lee·mee·teh

# Public Transportation

## Essential Information

- To ask directions to a bus stop, the bus station, a streetcar stop, the train station, a subway station, or a taxi stand, see p. 9.
- Remember that lining up for buses is unheard of!
- Taxis can be found at taxi stands in the main areas of a town, especially at the train station.
- Here are the different types of trains, listed according to speed (slowest to fastest).

| | |
|---|---|
| **Express** | Train that stops at both large and middle-sized cities |
| **Rapide** | Train that stops only at major cities |
| **Corail** | Air-conditioned intercity luxury train, usually with a dining car |
| **Trans Europe Express (TEE)** | Non-stop fast train between major European cities; first class only |
| **Train à Grande Vitesse (TGV)** | High-speed train serving over 150 cities in France and Switzerland |

- Here are signs to look for. (See also p. 108.)

| | |
|---|---|
| **Accès aux quais** | To the trains |
| **Arrêt d'autobus** | Bus stop |
| **Billets** | Tickets, ticket booth |
| **Consigne** | Luggage storage |
| **Entrée** | Entrance |
| **Interdit(e)** | Prohibited |
| **Locations** | Rentals |
| **Montée** | Entrance for buses |
| **N'oubliez pas de composter** | Remember to validate |
| **Renseignements** | Information |
| **Quai** | Platform |
| **Sortie** | Exit |
| **Voie** | Track, platform |

- You must validate your rail ticket by using one of the orange-colored date-stamping machines provided at platform entrances *before* departure. If you fail to do so, you will be liable for a fine of up to 20% of your fare.

  However, these regulations do not apply to international tickets purchased outside France.

- A supplement is an additional fee that is sometimes required if you want to buy a ticket for a train that has services (including speed) not included in the basic ticket price or in the Railpass price.

- There is a flat rate for subway tickets, and it is cheaper to buy a **carnet** (a book of ten tickets). In Paris, bus and subway tickets are interchangeable.

## What to Say

| | |
|---|---|
| Where does the train for (Paris) leave from? | **De quelle voie part le train de (Paris)?** <br> der kel vwah par ler tran der (pah·ree) |
| (At) what time does the train leave for (Paris)? | **À quelle heure part le train de (Paris)?** <br> ah kel er par ler tran der (pah·ree) |
| (At) what time does the train arrive in (Paris)? | **À quelle heure le train arrive-t-il à (Paris)?** <br> ah kel er ler tran ah·reev·teel ah (pah·ree) |
| Is this the train for (Paris)? | **Est-ce le train de (Paris)?** <br> es ler tran der (pah·ree) |
| Where does the bus for (Toulouse) leave from? | **D'où part l'autobus de (Toulouse)?** <br> doo par loh·toh·boos der (too·looz) |
| (At) what time does the bus leave for (Toulouse)? | **À quelle heure part l'autobus de (Toulouse)?** <br> ah kel er par loh·toh·boos der (too·looz) |
| (At) what time does the bus arrive in (Toulouse)? | **À quelle heure l'autobus arrive-t-il à (Toulouse)?** <br> ah kel er loh·toh·boos ah·reev·teel ah (too·looz) |
| Is this the bus for (Toulouse)? | **Est-ce l'autobus de (Toulouse)?** <br> es loh·toh·boos der (too·looz) |
| Do I have to change (trains)? | **Faut-il changer?** <br> foh·teel shahn·sheh |

| | |
|---|---|
| Where does … leave from? | **D'où part…**<br>doo par |
| … the bus … | **l'autobus**<br>loh·toh·boos |
| … the boat/ferry … | **le bateau/le ferry**<br>ler bah·toh/ler fair·ee |
| … the subway … | **le métro**<br>ler meh·troh |
| … the train … | **le train**<br>ler tran |
| … for the airport … | **pour l'aéroport?**<br>poor lah·eh·roh·por |
| … for the beach … | **pour la plage?**<br>poor lah plahsh |
| … for the cathedral … | **pour la cathédrale?**<br>poor lah cah·teh·drahl |
| … for downtown … | **pour le centre de la ville?**<br>poor ler sahnt der lah veel |
| … for the marketplace … | **pour la place du marché?**<br>poor lah plahss doo mar·sheh |
| … for (St. John's) Church … | **pour l'église (St Jean)?**<br>poor leh·gleez (san shahn) |
| … for the swimming pool … | **pour la piscine?**<br>poor lah pee·seen |
| … for the town hall … | **pour la mairie?**<br>poor lah mair·ee |
| … for the train station … | **pour la gare?**<br>poor lah gar |
| Is this … | **Est-ce…**<br>es |
| … the bus to the marketplace? | **l'autobus pour la place du marché?**<br>loh·toh·boos poor lah plahss doo mar·sheh |
| … the bus to the railway station? | **l'autobus pour le gare?**<br>loh·toh·boos poor lah gar |
| Where can I get a taxi? | **Où puis-je trouver un taxi?**<br>oo pweesh troo·veh an tahx·ee |
| Can you tell me when to get off, please? | **Pouvez-vous me dire où je dois descendre, s'il vous plaît?**<br>poo·veh·voo mer deer oo sher dwah deh·sahnd sil voo pleh |
| Can I reserve a seat? | **Puis-je réserver une place?**<br>pweesh reh·zair·veh oon plahss |

A one-way ticket.
**Un aller.**
  an ah·leh

A round-trip ticket.
**Un aller-retour.**
  an ah·leh rer·toor

First class.
**Première classe.**
  preh·myair clahss

Second class.
**Deuxième classe.**
  der·zee·em clahss

One adult …
**Un adulte…**
  an ah·doolt

Two adults …
**Deux adultes…**
  der·zah·doolt

… and one child.
**et un enfant.**
  eh an ahn·fahn

… and two children.
**et deux enfants.**
  eh der·zahn·fahn

How much is it?
**C'est combien?**
  seh com·bee·an

## Likely Reactions

Over there.
**Là-bas.**
  lah·bah

Here.
**Ici.**
  ee·see

Platform (1).
**Quai numéro (un)/(Première) voie.**
  keh noo·meh·roh (an)/(preh·myair)
  vwah

At (4 o'clock).
**À (quatre heures).**
  ah (kat er)

For telling time, see p. 114.

Change at (Vichy).
**Changez à (Vichy).**
  shahn·sheh ah (vee·shee)

Change at (the town hall).
**Changez à (la mairie).**
  shahn·sheh ah (lah mair·ee)

This is your stop.
**Voici votre arrêt.**
  vwah·see voht ah·reh

There is only first class.
**Il n'y a que des premières (classes).**
  il nee·yah ker deh preh·myair
  (clahss)

There's a supplement.
**Il y a un supplément.**
  il yah an soo·pleh·mahn

# Leisure and Entertainment

## Essential Information

- To ask directions to a place of entertainment, see p. 11.
- For telling time, see p. 114.
- For important signs, see p. 108.
- In the more popular seaside resorts, you have to pay to go onto the beach and to rent lounge chairs and beach umbrellas.
- Smoking is forbidden in movies and theaters, unless otherwise specified.

## What to Say

| | |
|---|---|
| (At) what time does … open? | **À quelle heure ouvre…**<br>ah kel er oov |
| (At) what time does … close? | **À quelle heure ferme…**<br>ah kel er fairm |
| … the art gallery … | **le musée d'art?**<br>ler moo·zeh dar |
| … the botanical garden … | **le jardin botanique?**<br>ler shar·dan boh·tah·neek |
| … the cinema … | **le cinéma?**<br>ler see·neh·mah |
| … the concert hall … | **la salle de concerts?**<br>lah sahl der cohn·sair |
| … the disco … | **la discothèque?**<br>lah dees·coh·tek |
| … the museum … | **le musée?**<br>ler moo·zeh |
| … the nightclub … | **la boîte de nuit?**<br>lah bwaht der nwee |
| … the sports stadium … | **le stade?**<br>ler stahd |
| … the swimming pool … | **la piscine?**<br>lah pee·seen |
| … the theater … | **le théâtre?**<br>ler teh·aht |
| … the zoo … | **le zoo?**<br>ler zoh·oh |

(At) what time does ... start?
**À quelle heure commence...**
ah kel er com·mahns

... the cabaret ...
**le cabaret?**
ler cah·bah·reh

... the concert ...
**le concert?**
ler cohn·sair

... the game/match ...
**le match?**
ler mahtch

... the movie ...
**le film?**
ler feelm

... the play ...
**la pièce?**
lah pee·ess

... the race ...
**la course?**
lah coorss

How much is it...
**C'est combien...**
seh com·bee·an

... for an adult?
**pour un adulte?**
poor an ah·doolt

... for a child?
**pour un enfant?**
poor an ahn·fahn

Two adults, please.
**Deux adultes, s'il vous plaît.**
der·zah·doolt sil voo pleh

Three children.
**Trois enfants.**
trwah·zahn·fahn

Orchestra/circle/sun/shade.
[*state the price, if there's a choice*]
**Orchestre/balcon/au soleil/ à l'ombre.**
or·kest/bahl·cohn/oh soh·leh/ ah lohmb

Do you have ...
**Avez-vous...**
ah·veh·voo

... a guidebook?
**un guide?**
an gheed

... a program?
**un programme?**
an proh·grahm

Where are the restrooms, please?
**Où sont les WC, s'il vous plaît?**
oo sohn leh veh·seh sil voo pleh

Where is the coatroom?
**Où est le vestiaire?**
oo eh ler ves·tyair

I would like lessons in ...
**Je voudrais des leçons de...**
sher voo·dreh deh leh·sohn der

... sailing.
**voile.**
vwahl

... scuba diving.
**plongée sous-marine.**
plon·sheh soo·mah·reen

| | |
|---|---|
| I would like lessons in … | **Je voudrais des leçons de…**<br>sher voo·dreh deh leh·sohn der |
| … skiing. | **ski.**<br>skee |
| … water skiing. | **ski nautique.**<br>skee noh·teek |
| Can I rent … | **Puis-je louer…**<br>pweesh loo·eh |
| … a beach umbrella? | **un parasol?**<br>an pah·rah·sohl |
| … a boat? | **un bateau?**<br>an bah·toh |
| … a lounge chair? | **une chaise-longue?**<br>oon shehz·long |
| … a fishing rod? | **une canne à pêche?**<br>oon cahn ah pesh |
| … some skis? | **des skis?**<br>deh skee |
| … some ski boots? | **des chaussures de ski?**<br>deh shoh·soor der skee |
| How much is it … | **C'est combien…**<br>seh com·bee·an |
| … per day? | **par jour?**<br>par shoor |
| … per hour? | **de l'heure?**<br>der ler |
| Do I need a license? | **Faut-il un permis?**<br>foh·teel an pair·mee |

# Asking If Things Are Allowed

## Essential Information

- The easiest way to ask if something is allowed is to use the French equivalent of "May one …?" (**On peut…?**). For example, to ask if you can smoke, say **On peut fumer ici?**

- This expression can be used to represent all the following questions.

  May one …?
  May I …?
  May we …?
  Can one …?
  Can I …?
  Can we …?
  Is it okay to …?

- To save space, only the first English version ("May one …?") is given below.

## What to Say

| | |
|---|---|
| Excuse me, please. | **Excusez-moi, s'il vous plaît.**<br>ex·coo·seh mwah sil voo pleh |
| May one … | **On peut…**<br>on per |
| … camp here? | **camper ici?**<br>cahm·peh ee·see |
| … come in? | **entrer?**<br>ahn·treh |
| … dance here? | **danser ici?**<br>dahn·seh ee·see |
| … fish here? | **pêcher ici?**<br>peh·sheh ee·see |
| … get a drink here? | **avoir des boissons ici?**<br>ah·vwah deh bwah·sohn ee·see |
| … get out this way? | **sortir par ici?**<br>sor·teer par ee·see |
| … get something to eat here? | **manger quelque chose ici?**<br>mahn·sheh kel·ker shohz ee·see |
| … leave one's things here? | **laisser ses affaires ici?**<br>leh·seh seh·zah·fair ee·see |
| … look around? | **regarder?**<br>rer·gar·deh |

| | |
|---|---|
| May one … | **On peut…**<br>on per |
| … make a telephone call here? | **téléphoner ici?**<br>teh·leh·foh·neh ee·see |
| … park here? | **se garer ici?**<br>ser gah·reh ee·see |
| … picnic here? | **pique-niquer ici?**<br>peek·neek·eh ee·see |
| … sit here? | **s'asseoir ici?**<br>sah·swah ee·see |
| … smoke here? | **fumer ici?**<br>foo·meh ee·see |
| … swim here? | **nager ici?**<br>nah·sheh ee·see |
| … take photos here? | **prendre des photos ici?**<br>prahnd deh foh·toh ee·see |
| … wait here? | **attendre ici?**<br>aht·tahnd ee·see |

## Likely Reactions

| | |
|---|---|
| Yes, certainly. | **Certainement.**<br>sair·ten·mahn |
| Help yourself. | **Allez-y.**<br>ah·leh·zee |
| I think so. | **Je crois.**<br>sher crwah |
| Of course. | **Bien sûr.**<br>bee·an soor |
| Yes, but be careful. | **Oui, mais faites attention.**<br>wee meh fet aht·tahn·syohn |
| No, certainly not. | **Certainement pas.**<br>sair·ten·mahn pah |
| I don't think so. | **Je ne crois pas.**<br>sher ner crwah pah |
| Not normally. | **Normalement, non.**<br>nor·mahl·mahn nohn |
| Sorry. | **Je regrette.**<br>sher rer·gret |

# Reference

## Public Notices

**Signs for Drivers, Pedestrians, Travelers, Shoppers, and Overnight Guests**

| | |
|---|---|
| À louer | For rent |
| À vendre | For sale |
| Accotements non stabilisés | Soft shoulders |
| Allumez vos phares | Turn lights on |
| Appuyer ici | Press here |
| Arrivées | Arrivals |
| Ascenseur | Elevator |
| Attendez | Wait |
| Attention | Caution |
| Attention—chien méchant | Beware of the dog |
| Attention aux trains | Caution: Trains |
| Autoroute | Highway |
| Baignade interdite | No swimming |
| Bière pression | Draft beer |
| Billets | Tickets |
| Brocante | Secondhand/junk shop; flea market |
| Caisse | Cashier, teller |
| Camping interdit | No camping |
| Centre ville | Downtown |
| Chambre à louer | Room to rent |
| Chambres libres | Vacancies |
| Chaud | Hot (water) |
| Chaussée défoncée | Bad surface [road] |
| Chaussée glissante | Slippery surface [road] |
| Chaussée rétrécie | Road narrows |
| Chute de pierres | Falling rocks |
| Circuit touristique | Scenic route |
| Clés-minute | Keys cut while you wait |
| Complet | Full—no vacancies |
| Congé annuel | Closed for the holidays |
| Consigne | Luggage storage |
| Cyclistes | Bicyclists |
| Dames | Ladies |
| Défense d'afficher | No bill posting |
| Défense d'entrer sous peine d'amende | Trespassers will be prosecuted |

| | |
|---|---|
| **Dépannage** | Emergency repairs |
| **Départs** | Departures |
| **Déviation** | Detour |
| **Douche** | Shower |
| **Eau non potable** | Not for drinking (water) |
| **Eau potable** | Drinking water |
| **École** | School |
| **Empruntez le souterrain** | Take the subway |
| **En réclame** | Special offer |
| **Entrée** | Entrance |
| **Entrée gratuite** | Free entry |
| **Entrée interdite** | No entry |
| **Escalier** | Stairs |
| **Étage (premier, deuxième)** | Floor (first, second) |
| **Femmes** | Ladies |
| **Fermé (le lundi)** | Closed (on Mondays) |
| **Fermeture annuelle** | Closed for the holidays |
| **Feux de circulation** | Traffic lights |
| **File de droite** | Right-hand lane |
| **File de gauche** | Left-hand lane |
| **Fin d'autoroute** | End of highway |
| **Frappez** | Knock |
| **Froid** | Cold (water) |
| **Gare routière** | Bus station |
| **Gare SNCF** | Train station |
| **Gratuit** | Free |
| **Hôpital** | Hospital |
| **Il est interdit de doubler** | No passing |
| **Il est interdit de fumer** | No smoking |
| **Impasse** | Dead end |
| **Interdit** | Prohibited |
| **Interdit aux piétons** | No pedestrians |
| **Introduisez votre pièce ici** | Insert coin here |
| **Jour de fermeture** | Closing day |
| **Lavabos** | Restrooms |
| **Laverie automatique** | Laundromat |
| **Libre** | Free |
| **Location (de voitures)** | (Car) Rental |
| **Locations** | Rentals |
| **Messieurs** | Gentlemen |
| **Métro** | Subway |
| **Nettoyage à sec, pressing** | Dry cleaning |

| | |
|---|---|
| **Objets trouvés** | Lost and found |
| **Occasions** | Bargains |
| **Occupé** | Occupied |
| **Ouvert** | Open |
| **Parking** | Parking |
| **Parler ici** | Speak here |
| **Passage à niveau** | Grade crossing |
| **Passage souterrain** | Subway |
| **Payez à la sortie** | Pay on your way out |
| **Payez ici** | Pay here |
| **Péage** | Toll |
| **Piétons** | Pedestrians |
| **Places debout** | Standing room |
| **Poids lourds** | Heavy trucks |
| **Porteur** | Porter |
| **Poussez** | Push |
| **Prière de ne pas (toucher)** | Please do not (touch) |
| **Priorité (à droite)** | Right of way (on the right) |
| **Privé** | Private |
| **Propriété privée** | Private property |
| **Quai** | Platform/dock |
| **Ralentir** | Slow down |
| **Relâche** | Closed [*theaters, cinemas*] |
| **Remises** | Discounts |
| **Renseignements** | Information |
| **Réservé aux autobus** | Buses only |
| **Réservé aux cyclistes** | Bicycle lane |
| **Respectez les pelouses** | Keep off the grass |
| **Rez-de-chaussée** | Ground floor |
| **Sables mouvants** | Quicksand |
| **Salle à manger** | Dining room |
| **Salle d'attente** | Waiting room |
| **Sens unique** | One-way street |
| **Serrez à droite** | Keep right |
| **Soldes** | Sales |
| **Sonnez** | Ring [*doorbell*] |
| **Sortie** | Exit |
| **Sortie d'autoroute** | Highway exit |
| **Sortie de camions** | Truck exit |
| **Sortie de secours** | Emergency exit |
| **Sous-sol** | Basement |
| **Stationnement interdit** | No parking |

| | |
|---|---|
| **Stationnement jours impairs** | Parking allowed on odd days of the month |
| **Stationnement limité** | Parking allowed on even days of the month |
| **Syndicat d'initiative** | Tourist information office |
| **Terrain militaire** | Military zone |
| **Tirez** | Pull |
| **Toilettes** | Restrooms |
| **Tournez la poignée** | Turn the handle |
| **Toutes directions** | Through traffic |
| **Travaux** | Roadwork |
| **Traversez** | Cross |
| **TVA en sus** | Plus tax |
| **Ventes** | Sales |
| **Virages** | Curves |
| **Vitesse limitée** | Speed limit |
| **Voie** | Platform/track |
| **Voie sans issue** | Dead-end street |
| **WC** | Restrooms |
| **Zone bleue** | Parking permits required |
| **Zone piétonnière** | Pedestrian area |

## Abbreviations

| | | |
|---|---|---|
| A | autoroute | highway |
| AJ | **Auberge de jeunesse** | youth hostel |
| arr. | arrondissement | administrative district |
| C | chaude | hot (water faucet) |
| CFF | **Chemins de Fer Fédéraux** | Swiss rail |
| ch.-l | chef-lieu | principal town in district |
| cl | centilitre | centiliter |
| D | (route) départementale | secondary road |
| dep. | département | administrative county |
| douz. | douzaine | dozen |
| EGDF | **Électricité et Gaz de France** | French Electricity and Gas |
| E.U. | États-Unis | United States |
| € | euro | euro |
| F | fermé | off |
| | franc | franc |
| | froid | cold (water faucet) |
| faub. | faubourg | suburb |
| HT | haute tension | high voltage |

| | | |
|---|---|---|
| k/kg(s) | **kilogramme(s)** | kilogram(s) |
| km | **kilomètre** | kilometer |
| L | **Livre sterling** | British pound |
| l | **litre** | liter |
| M/MM | **Monsieur/Messieurs** | Mr./Messrs. |
| Mlle/<br> Mlles | **Mademoiselle/<br> Mesdemoiselles** | Miss/the Misses |
| Mme/<br> Mmes | **Madame/Mesdames** | Mrs./Mesdames |
| N | **(route) nationale** | main highway |
| O | **Ouvert** | on |
| PT | **Postes et<br> Télécommunications** | post office |
| RD | **Route départementale** | secondary road |
| RER | **Réseau express régional** | express trains |
| RF | **République française** | French Republic |
| RN | **Route nationale** | main road |
| SI | **Syndicat d'initiative** | tourist information office |
| SNCB | **Société Nationale des<br> Chemins de Fer Belges** | Belgian Rail |
| SNCF | **Société Nationale des<br> Chemins de Fer Français** | French Rail |
| s.pref. | **sous-préfecture** | important town in a<br> *département* |
| SS | **Sécurité Sociale** | Social Security/National<br> Health |
| THT | **Très haute tension** | Very high voltage |
| TSVP | **Tournez s'il vous plaît** | Please turn over |
| t.t.c. | **toutes taxes comprises** | tax included |
| TVA | **Taxe à la valeur ajoutée** | value-added tax (VAT) |

# Numbers

## Cardinal Numbers

| | | |
|---|---|---|
| 0 | **zéro** | zeh-roh |
| 1 | **un** | an |
| 2 | **deux** | der |
| 3 | **trois** | trwah |
| 4 | **quatre** | kat |
| 5 | **cinq** | sank |
| 6 | **six** | seess |

| | | |
|---|---|---|
| 7 | **sept** | set |
| 8 | **huit** | weet |
| 9 | **neuf** | nerf |
| 10 | **dix** | deess |
| 11 | **onze** | ohnz |
| 12 | **douze** | dooz |
| 13 | **treize** | trez |
| 14 | **quatorze** | kat-torz |
| 15 | **quinze** | kanz |
| 16 | **seize** | sez |
| 17 | **dix-sept** | dee-set |
| 18 | **dix-huit** | deez-weet |
| 19 | **dix-neuf** | deez-nerf |
| 20 | **vingt** | van |
| 21 | **vingt et un** | van-teh an |
| 22 | **vingt-deux** | vant-der |
| 23 | **vingt-trois** | vant-trwah |
| 24 | **vingt-quatre** | vant-kat |
| 25 | **vingt-cinq** | vant-sank |
| 26 | **vingt-six** | vant-seess |
| 27 | **vingt-sept** | vant-set |
| 28 | **vingt-huit** | vant-weet |
| 29 | **vingt-neuf** | vant-nerf |
| 30 | **trente** | trahnt |
| 31 | **trente et un** | trahnt-teh an |
| 35 | **trente-cinq** | trahnt-sank |
| 38 | **trente-huit** | trahnt-weet |
| 40 | **quarante** | kah-rahnt |
| 41 | **quarante et un** | kah-rahn-teh an |
| 45 | **quarante-cinq** | kah-rahnt-sank |
| 48 | **quarante-huit** | kah-rahnt-weet |
| 50 | **cinquante** | sank-ahnt |
| 55 | **cinquante-cinq** | sank-ahnt-sank |
| 60 | **soixante** | swah-sahnt |
| 65 | **soixante-cinq** | swah-sahnt-sank |
| 70 | **soixante-dix** | swah-sahnt-deess |
| 75 | **soixante-quinze** | swah-sahnt-kanz |
| 80 | **quatre-vingts** | kat van |
| 85 | **quatre-vingt-cinq** | kat vant-sank |
| 90 | **quatre-vingt-dix** | kat vant-deess |
| 95 | **quatre-vingt-quinze** | kat vant-kanz |
| 100 | **cent** | sahn |

| 101 | **cent un** | sahn an |
| 102 | **cent deux** | sahn der |
| 125 | **cent vingt-cinq** | sahn vant-sank |
| 150 | **cent cinquante** | sahn sank-ahnt |
| 175 | **cent soixante-quinze** | sahn swah-sahnt-kanz |
| 200 | **deux cents** | der sahn |
| 300 | **trois cents** | trwah sahn |
| 400 | **quatre cents** | kat sahn |
| 500 | **cinq cents** | sank sahn |
| 1,000 | **mille** | meel |
| 1,500 | **mille cinq cents** | meel sank sahn |
| 2,000 | **deux mille** | der meel |
| 5,000 | **cinq mille** | sank meel |
| 10,000 | **dix mille** | dee meel |
| 100,000 | **cent mille** | sahn meel |
| 1,000,000 | **un million** | an meel-yohn |

## Ordinal Numbers

| 1st | **premier (1er)** | preh-myeh |
| 2nd | **deuxième (2e)** | derz-yem |
| 3rd | **troisième (3e)** | trwahz-yem |
| 4th | **quatrième (4e)** | katr-yem |
| 5th | **cinquième (5e)** | sank-yem |
| 6th | **sixième (6e)** | seess-yem |
| 7th | **septième (7e)** | set-yem |
| 8th | **huitième (8e)** | weet-yem |
| 9th | **neuvième (9e)** | nerf-yem |
| 10th | **dixième (10e)** | deez-yem |
| 11th | **onzième (11e)** | onhz-yem |
| 12th | **douzième (12e)** | dooz-yem |

# Time

| What time is it? | **Quelle heure est-il?** |
| | kel er eh·teel |
| It is one o'clock. | **Il est une heure.** |
| | il eh·toon er |
| It is … | **Il est…** |
| | il eh |
| … two o'clock … | **deux heures** |
| | der·zer |

| It is … | **Il est…** |
| | il eh |
| … three o'clock … | **trois heures** |
| | trwah·zer |
| … four o'clock … | **quatre heures** |
| | kat·rer |
| … in the morning. | **du matin.** |
| | doo mah·tan |
| … in the afternoon. | **de l'après-midi.** |
| | der lah·preh·mee·dee |
| … in the evening. | **du soir.** |
| | doo swah |
| It is … | **Il est…** |
| | il eh |
| … noon. | **midi.** |
| | mee·dee |
| … midnight. | **minuit.** |
| | mee·nwee |
| It is … | **Il est…** |
| | il eh |
| … five past five. | **cinq heures cinq.** |
| | sank er sank |
| … ten past five. | **cinq heures dix.** |
| | sank er deess |
| … a quarter past five. | **cinq heures et quart.** |
| | sank er eh car |
| … twenty past five. | **cinq heures vingt.** |
| | sank er van |
| … twenty-five past five. | **cinq heures vingt-cinq.** |
| | sank er vant·sank |
| … half past five. | **cinq heures et demie.** |
| | sank er eh der·mee |
| … twenty-five to six. | **six heures moins vingt-cinq.** |
| | see·zer mwen vant·sank |
| … twenty to six. | **six heures moins vingt.** |
| | see·zer mwen van |
| … a quarter to six. | **six heures moins le quart.** |
| | see·zer mwen ler car |
| … ten to six. | **six heures moins dix.** |
| | see·zer mwen deess |
| … five to six. | **six heures moins cinq.** |
| | see·zer mwen sank |

| | |
|---|---|
| (At) what time (does the train leave)? | **À quelle heure (part le train)?** <br> ah kel er (par ler tran) |
| At … | **À…** <br> ah |
| … 13:00. | **treize heures.** <br> trez·er |
| … 14:05. | **quatorze heures zéro cinq.** <br> kat·tor·zer zeh·roh sank |
| … 15:10. | **quinze heures dix.** <br> kan·zer deess |
| … 16:15. | **seize heures quinze.** <br> sez·er kanz |
| … 17:20. | **dix-sept heures vingt.** <br> dee·set er van |
| … 18:25. | **dix-huit heures vingt-cinq.** <br> deez·weet er vant·sank |
| … 19:30. | **dix-neuf heures trente.** <br> deez·nerf er trahnt |
| … 20:35. | **vingt heures trente-cinq.** <br> vant er trahnt·sank |
| … 21:40. | **vingt et une heures quarante.** <br> vant eh oon er kah·rahnt |
| … 22:45. | **vingt-deux heures quarante-cinq.** <br> vant·der·zer kah·rahnt·sank |
| … 23:50. | **vingt-trois heures cinquante.** <br> vant·trwah·zer sank·ahnt |
| … 00:55. | **zéro heure cinquante-cinq.** <br> zeh·roh er sank·ahnt·sank |
| In ten minutes. | **Dans dix minutes.** <br> dahn dee mee·noot |
| In a quarter of an hour. | **Dans un quart d'heure.** <br> dahn·zan car der |
| In half an hour. | **Dans une demi-heure.** <br> dahn·zoon der·mee·er |
| In three quarters of an hour. | **Dans trois quarts d'heure.** <br> dahn trwah car der |

# Days

| | |
|---|---|
| Monday | **lundi** <br> lern·dee |
| Tuesday | **mardi** <br> mar·dee |

| Wednesday | **mercredi** |
| | mairk·rdee |
| Thursday | **jeudi** |
| | sher·dee |
| Friday | **vendredi** |
| | vahn·drer·dee |
| Saturday | **samedi** |
| | sahm·dee |
| Sunday | **dimanche** |
| | dee·mahnsh |
| last Monday | **lundi dernier** |
| | lern·dee dair·nyeh |
| next Tuesday | **mardi prochain** |
| | mar·dee proh·shan |
| on Wednesday | **mercredi** |
| | mairk·rdee |
| on Thursdays | **le jeudi** |
| | ler sher·dee |
| until Friday | **jusqu'à vendredi** |
| | shoosh·kah vahn·drer·dee |
| before Saturday | **avant samedi** |
| | ah·vahn sahm·dee |
| after Sunday | **après dimanche** |
| | ah·preh dee·mahnsh |
| the day before yesterday | **avant-hier** |
| | ah·vahn·tee·air |
| two days ago | **il y a deux jours** |
| | il yah der shoor |
| yesterday | **hier** |
| | ee·air |
| yesterday morning | **hier matin** |
| | ee·air mah·tan |
| yesterday afternoon | **hier après-midi** |
| | ee·air ah·preh·mee·dee |
| last night (evening) | **hier soir** |
| | ee·air swah |
| today | **aujourd'hui** |
| | oh·shoor·dwee |
| this morning | **ce matin** |
| | ser mah·tan |
| this afternoon | **cet après-midi** |
| | set ah·preh·mee·dee |
| tonight | **ce soir** |
| | ser swah |

| | |
|---|---|
| tomorrow | **demain**<br>der·man |
| tomorrow morning | **demain matin**<br>der·man mah·tan |
| tomorrow evening/tomorrow night | **demain soir**<br>der·man swah |
| the day after tomorrow | **après-demain**<br>ah·preh·der·man |

## Months, Dates, Seasons, and Years

| | |
|---|---|
| January | **janvier**<br>shahn·vyeh |
| February | **février**<br>feh·vree·eh |
| March | **mars**<br>marss |
| April | **avril**<br>ah·vreel |
| May | **mai**<br>meh |
| June | **juin**<br>shoo·an |
| July | **juillet**<br>shwee·yeh |
| August | **août**<br>oot |
| September | **septembre**<br>sep·tahmb |
| October | **octobre**<br>ohk·tohb |
| November | **novembre**<br>noh·vahmb |
| December | **décembre**<br>deh·sahmb |
| in January | **au mois de janvier**<br>oh mwah der shahn·vyeh |
| until February | **jusqu'au mois de février**<br>shoo·skoh mwah der feh·vree·eh |
| before March | **avant le mois de mars**<br>ah·vahn ler mwah der marss |
| after April | **après le mois d'avril**<br>ah·preh ler mwah dah·vreel |

| | |
|---|---|
| during May | **pendant le mois de mai**<br>pahn·dahn ler mwah der meh |
| not until June | **pas avant le mois de juin**<br>pah·zah·vahn ler mwah der shoo·an |
| the beginning of July | **le début juillet**<br>ler deh·boo shwee·yeh |
| the middle of August | **la mi-août**<br>lah mee·oot |
| the end of September | **la fin septembre**<br>lah fan sep·tahmb |
| last month | **le mois dernier**<br>ler mwah dair·nyeh |
| this month | **ce mois-ci**<br>ser mwah·see |
| next month | **le mois prochain**<br>ler mwah proh·shan |
| in the spring | **au printemps**<br>oh pran·tahn |
| in the summer | **en été**<br>ahn eh·teh |
| in the fall/autumn | **en automne**<br>ahn oh·tohn |
| in the winter | **en hiver**<br>ahn ee·vair |
| this year | **cette année**<br>set ah·neh |
| last year | **l'année dernière**<br>lah·neh dair·nyair |
| next year | **l'année prochaine**<br>lah·neh proh·shen |
| in 1985 | **en mil neuf cent quatre-vingt-cinq**<br>ahn meel nerf sahn kat·vant·sank |
| in 1990 | **en mil neuf cent quatre-vingt-dix**<br>ahn meel nerf sahn kat·vant·deess |
| in 2000 | **en l'an deux mille**<br>ahn lahn der meel |
| in 2006 | **en l'an deux mille six**<br>ahn lahn der meel seess |
| What is the date today? | **Quel jour sommes-nous?**<br>kel shoor som·noo |
| It is the 6th of March. | **C'est le six mars.**<br>seh ler see marss |

| | |
|---|---|
| It is the 12th of April. | **C'est le douze avril.** |
| | seh ler doo·zah·vreel |
| It is the 21st of August. | **C'est le vingt et un août.** |
| | seh le vant eh an oot |

# Public Holidays in France and Belgium

Bank, post offices, public offices, retail stores, and schools are closed on the following holidays.

| | | |
|---|---|---|
| January 1 | **Jour de l'An** | New Year's Day |
| [*varies*] | **Lundi de Pâques** | Easter Monday |
| May 1 | **Fête du Travail** | Labor Day |
| [*varies*] | **Ascension** | Ascension Day |
| [*varies*] | **Lundi de Pentecôte** | Monday following Pentecost |
| July 14 | **Quatorze Juillet** | Bastille Day (France) |
| July 21 | **Fête Nationale** | National Day (Belgium) |
| August 15 | **Assomption Quinze Août** | Assumption Day |
| November 1 | **Toussaint** | All Saints Day |
| November 11 | **Armistice** | Armistice Day |
| December 25 | **Noël** | Christmas Day |
| December 26 | **Saint-Étienne** | St. Stephen's Day (Belgium) |

# Countries and Nationalities

## Countries

| | |
|---|---|
| Australia | **(l')Australie** |
| | (l)oh·strah·lee |
| Austria | **(l')Autriche** |
| | (l)oh·treesh |
| Belgium | **(la) Belgique** |
| | (lah) bel·sheek |
| Britain | **(la) Grande-Bretagne** |
| | (lah) grahnd breh·tahn |
| Canada | **(le) Canada** |
| | (ler) cah·nah·dah |
| East Africa | **(l')Afrique de l'Est** |
| | (l)ah·freek der lest |
| Eire | **(l')Irlande** |
| | (l)eer·lahnd |

| England | **(l')Angleterre** |
| | (l)ahng·tair |
| France | **(la) France** |
| | (lah) frahns |
| Germany | **(l')Allemagne** |
| | (l)ahl·mahn |
| Greece | **(la) Grèce** |
| | (lah) gress |
| India | **(l')Inde** |
| | (l)and |
| Italy | **(l')Italie** |
| | (l)ee·tah·lee |
| Luxembourg | **(le) Luxembourg** |
| | (ler) look·sahn·boor |
| Netherlands | **(la) Hollande** |
| | (lah) oh·lahnd |
| New Zealand | **(la) Nouvelle Zélande** |
| | (lah) noo·vel zeh·lahnd |
| Northern Ireland | **(l')Irlande du Nord** |
| | (l)eer·lahnd doo nor |
| Pakistan | **(le) Pakistan** |
| | (ler) pah·kee·stan |
| Portugal | **(le) Portugal** |
| | (ler) por·too·gahl |
| Scotland | **(l')Écosse** |
| | (l)eh·coss |
| South Africa | **(l')Afrique du Sud** |
| | (l)ah·freek doo sood |
| Spain | **(l')Espagne** |
| | (l)eh·spahn |
| Switzerland | **(la) Suisse** |
| | (lah) sweess |
| United States | **(les) États-Unis** |
| | (lehz) eh·tah·zoo·nee |
| Wales | **(le) Pays de Galles** |
| | (ler) peh·ee der gahl |
| West Indies | **(les) Antilles** |
| | (lehz) ahn·tee |
| in England | **en Angleterre** |
| | ahn ahng·tair |
| in Switzerland | **en Suisse** |
| | ahn sweess |

| | |
|---|---|
| in Pakistan | **au Pakistan** |
| | oh·pah·kee·stan |
| in Portugal | **au Portugal** |
| | oh por·too·gahl |
| in the United States | **aux États-Unis** |
| | oh·zeh·tah·zoo·nee |
| in the West Indies | **aux Antilles** |
| | oh·zahn·tee |

## Nationalities

Where two alternatives are given, the first is used for males, the second for females.

| | |
|---|---|
| American | **américain/américaine** |
| | ah·meh·ree·can/ah·meh·ree·ken |
| Australian | **australien/australienne** |
| | oh·strahl·yan/oh·strahl·yen |
| British | **britannique** |
| | bree·tah·neek |
| Canadian | **canadien/canadienne** |
| | cah·nah·dyan/cah·nah·dyen |
| East African | **est-africain/est-africaine** |
| | est·ah·free·can/est·ah·free·ken |
| English | **anglais/anglaise** |
| | ahn·gleh/ahn·glez |
| Indian | **indien/indienne** |
| | an·dyan/an·dyen |
| Irish | **irlandais/irlandaise** |
| | eer·lahn·deh/eer·lahn·dez |
| New Zealander | **néo-zélandais/néo-zélandaise** |
| | neh·oh·zeh·lahn·deh/ |
| | neh·oh·zeh·lahn·dez |
| Pakistani | **pakistanais/pakistanaise** |
| | pah·kee·stahn·eh/pah·kee·stahn·ez |
| Scots | **écossais/écossaise** |
| | eh·coh·seh/eh·coh·sez |
| South African | **sud-africain/sud-africaine** |
| | soo·dah·free·can/soo·dah·free·ken |
| Welsh | **gallois/galloise** |
| | gahl·wah/gahl·wahz |
| West Indian | **antillais/antillaise** |
| | ahn·tee·yeh/ahn·tee·yez |

# Department Store Guide

| | |
|---|---|
| **Accessoires automobile** | Car accessories |
| **Accessoires cuisine** | Kitchen gadgets |
| **Accessoires mode** | Fashion accessories |
| **Alimentation** | Food |
| **Ameublement** | Furniture |
| **Articles de mode** | Fashion items |
| **Articles de voyage** | Travel articles |
| **Arts ménagers** | Household items |
| **Bas** | Stockings |
| **Bijouterie** | Jewelry |
| **Blanc** | Linens |
| **Bricolage** | Do-it-yourself |
| **Cadeaux** | Gifts |
| **Caisse** | Cashier |
| **Camping** | Camping |
| **Ceintures** | Belts |
| **Chaussures** | Shoes |
| **Chemiserie** | Shirt department |
| **Chemises** | Shirts |
| **Confection** | Ready-to-wear |
| **Coussins** | Cushions |
| **Couvertures** | Blankets |
| **Cravates** | Ties |
| **Crédits** | Credit accounts |
| **Dame(s)** | Women's wear |
| **Deuxième** | Second |
| **Disques** | Music |
| **Éclairage** | Lighting |
| **Électroménager** | Electrical appliances |
| **Enfant(s)** | Children's |
| **Entretien** | Cleaning goods |
| **Étage** | Floor |
| **Gaines** | Girdles |
| **Homme(s)** | Men's wear |
| **Jouets** | Toys |
| **Layette** | Infant clothing |
| **Librairie** | Books |
| **Linge maison** | Household linens |
| **Lingerie** | Women's lingerie |
| **Literie** | Bedding |

| | |
|---|---|
| **Maquillage** | Makeup |
| **Maroquinerie** | Leather goods |
| **Mercerie** | Men's accessories |
| **Meubles de cuisine** | Kitchen furniture |
| **Meubles** | Furniture |
| **Mode(s)** | Fashions |
| **Pantoufles** | Slippers |
| **Papeterie** | Stationery |
| **Parfumerie** | Perfume |
| **Photo(graphie)** | Photography |
| **Premier** | First |
| **Prêt-à-porter** | Ready-to-wear |
| **Produits de beauté** | Beauty products |
| **Pulls** | Sweaters |
| **Quatrième** | Fourth |
| **Quincaillerie** | Hardware |
| **Radio** | Radio |
| **Renseignements** | Information |
| **Revêtements de sol** | Floor coverings |
| **Rez-de-chaussée** | Ground floor |
| **Rideaux** | Curtains |
| **Service après-vente** | Complaints, repairs |
| **Sous-sol** | Basement |
| **Sous-vêtements** | Underwear |
| **Soutiens-gorge** | Bras |
| **Tapis** | Carpets |
| **Télévision** | Television |
| **Tissus** | Fabrics |
| **Tissus d'ameublement** | Upholstery fabrics |
| **Troisième** | Third |
| **Vaisselle** | China |
| **Verrerie** | Glassware |

# Conversion Tables

## Metric/U.S. Systems

To convert from the metric to the U.S. system, read from the single digit in the center column to the number on the left; for example, 5 liters = 10.55 pints. To convert from the U.S. system to the metric, read from the single digit in the center column to the number on the right; for example, 5 pints = 2.35 liters.

| PINTS | | LITERS | GALLONS | | LITERS |
|---|---|---|---|---|---|
| 2.11 | 1 | 0.47 | 0.26 | 1 | 3.78 |
| 4.22 | 2 | 0.94 | 0.52 | 2 | 7.57 |
| 6.33 | 3 | 1.41 | 0.78 | 3 | 11.34 |
| 8.44 | 4 | 1.88 | 1.04 | 4 | 15.12 |
| 10.55 | 5 | 2.35 | 1.30 | 5 | 17.40 |
| 12.66 | 6 | 2.82 | 1.56 | 6 | 22.68 |
| 14.77 | 7 | 3.29 | 1.82 | 7 | 26.46 |
| 16.88 | 8 | 3.76 | 2.08 | 8 | 30.24 |
| 18.99 | 9 | 4.23 | 2.34 | 9 | 34.02 |

| OUNCES | | GRAMS | POUNDS | | KILOS |
|---|---|---|---|---|---|
| 0.04 | 1 | 28.35 | 2.20 | 1 | 0.45 |
| 0.07 | 2 | 56.70 | 4.41 | 2 | 0.91 |
| 0.11 | 3 | 85.05 | 6.61 | 3 | 1.36 |
| 0.14 | 4 | 113.40 | 8.82 | 4 | 1.81 |
| 0.18 | 5 | 141.75 | 11.02 | 5 | 2.27 |
| 0.21 | 6 | 170.10 | 13.23 | 6 | 2.72 |
| 0.25 | 7 | 198.45 | 15.43 | 7 | 3.18 |
| 0.28 | 8 | 226.80 | 17.64 | 8 | 3.63 |
| 0.32 | 9 | 255.15 | 19.84 | 9 | 4.08 |

| INCHES | | CENTIMETERS | YARDS | | METERS |
|---|---|---|---|---|---|
| 0.39 | 1 | 2.54 | 1.09 | 1 | 0.91 |
| 0.79 | 2 | 5.08 | 2.19 | 2 | 1.83 |
| 1.18 | 3 | 7.62 | 3.28 | 3 | 2.74 |
| 1.58 | 4 | 10.16 | 4.37 | 4 | 3.66 |
| 1.95 | 5 | 12.70 | 5.47 | 5 | 4.57 |
| 2.36 | 6 | 15.24 | 6.56 | 6 | 5.49 |
| 2.76 | 7 | 17.78 | 7.66 | 7 | 6.40 |
| 3.15 | 8 | 20.32 | 8.65 | 8 | 7.32 |
| 3.54 | 9 | 22.86 | 9.84 | 9 | 8.23 |

| MILES | | KILOMETERS |
|---|---|---|
| 0.62 | 1 | 1.61 |
| 1.24 | 2 | 3.22 |
| 1.86 | 3 | 4.83 |
| 2.49 | 4 | 6.44 |
| 3.11 | 5 | 8.05 |
| 3.73 | 6 | 9.66 |
| 4.35 | 7 | 11.27 |
| 4.97 | 8 | 12.87 |
| 5.59 | 9 | 14.48 |

To convert kilometers to miles, divide by 8 and multiply by 5. To convert miles to kilometers, divide by 5 and multiply by 8.

## Temperature

| FAHRENHEIT (° F) | CELSIUS (° C) | |
|---|---|---|
| 212° | 100° | boiling point of water |
| 100° | 38° | |
| 98.6° | 37° | body temperature |
| 86° | 30° | |
| 77° | 25° | |
| 68° | 20° | |
| 59° | 15° | |
| 50° | 10° | |
| 41° | 5° | |
| 32° | 0° | freezing point of water |
| 14° | −10° | |
| −4° | −20° | |

To convert degrees Celsius to degrees Fahrenheit, divide by 5, multiply by 9, and add 32. To convert degrees Fahrenheit to degrees Celsius, subtract 32, divide by 9, and multiply by 5.

## Tire Pressure

| POUNDS PER SQUARE INCH | KILOGRAMS PER SQUARE CENTIMETER |
|---|---|
| 18 | 1.3 |
| 20 | 1.4 |
| 22 | 1.5 |
| 25 | 1.7 |
| 29 | 2.0 |
| 32 | 2.3 |

| POUNDS PER SQUARE INCH | KILOGRAMS PER SQUARE CENTIMETER |
|---|---|
| 35 | 2.5 |
| 36 | 2.5 |
| 39 | 2.7 |
| 40 | 2.8 |
| 43 | 3.0 |
| 45 | 3.2 |
| 46 | 3.2 |
| 50 | 3.5 |
| 60 | 4.2 |

# Clothing Sizes

Always try clothes on before buying. Clothing sizes in conversion tables are often unreliable.

## Women's Dresses and Suits

| Continental Europe | 38 | 40 | 42 | 44 | 46 | 48 |
|---|---|---|---|---|---|---|
| U.K. | 32 | 34 | 36 | 38 | 40 | 42 |
| U.S. | 10 | 12 | 14 | 16 | 18 | 20 |

## Men's Suits, Coats, and Jackets

| Continental Europe | 46 | 48 | 50 | 52 | 54 | 56 |
|---|---|---|---|---|---|---|
| U.K./U.S. | 36 | 38 | 40 | 42 | 44 | 46 |

## Men's Shirts

| Continental Europe | 36 | 37 | 38 | 39 | 41 | 42 | 43 |
|---|---|---|---|---|---|---|---|
| U.K./U.S. | 14 | $14^{1}/_{2}$ | 15 | $15^{1}/_{2}$ | 16 | $16^{1}/_{2}$ | 17 |

## Socks

| Continental Europe | 38–39 | 39–40 | 40–41 | 41–42 | 42–43 |
|---|---|---|---|---|---|
| U.K./U.S. | $9^{1}/_{2}$ | 10 | $10^{1}/_{2}$ | 11 | $11^{1}/_{2}$ |

## Shoes

| Continental Europe | 34 | $35^{1}/_{2}$ | $36^{1}/_{2}$ | 38 | 39 |
|---|---|---|---|---|---|
| U.K. | 2 | 3 | 4 | 5 | 6 |
| U.S. | $3^{1}/_{2}$ | $4^{1}/_{2}$ | $5^{1}/_{2}$ | $6^{1}/_{2}$ | $7^{1}/_{2}$ |

| Continental Europe | 41 | 42 | 43 | 44 | 45 |
|---|---|---|---|---|---|
| U.K. | 7 | 8 | 9 | 10 | 11 |
| U.S. | $8^{1}/_{2}$ | $9^{1}/_{2}$ | $10^{1}/_{2}$ | $11^{1}/_{2}$ | $12^{1}/_{2}$ |

# Do It Yourself: Some Notes on the French Language

This section does not deal with "grammar" as such. The purpose here is to explain some of the most useful and elementary nuts and bolts of the language, based on the principal phrases included in the book. This information should enable you to produce numerous sentences of your own making.

There is no pronunciation guide in most of this section, partly because it would get in the way of the explanations and partly because you have to do it yourself at this stage if you are serious. You can use the earlier examples in this book to figure out the pronunciation of the French words in this section.

## "The"

All nouns in French belong to one of two genders—masculine or feminine—regardless of whether they refer to living beings or inanimate objects.

| "the" (SINGULAR) | MASCULINE | FEMININE |
|---|---|---|
| the address | | **l'adresse** |
| the apple | | **la pomme** |
| the bill | | **l'addition** |
| the cup of tea | | **la tasse de thé** |
| the glass of beer | **le verre de bière** | |
| the key | | **la clé** |
| the luggage | (*no singular*) | |
| the menu | **le menu** | |
| the newspaper | **le journal** | |
| the receipt | **le reçu** | |
| the sandwich | **le sandwich** | |
| the suitcase | | **la valise** |
| the telephone directory | **l'annuaire téléphonique** | |
| the schedule | **l'horaire** | |

• "The" is **le** before a masculine noun and **la** before a feminine noun.

- "The" is **l'** before masculine and feminine nouns that begin with a vowel (*h* often counts as a vowel): **l'adresse** (*feminine*) and **l'horaire** (*masculine*), when referring to a single thing.

- There is no way of predicting whether a noun is masculine or feminine, so you should learn the gender of nouns as you learn the nouns themselves. If you read a word with **le** or **la** in front of it, you can detect its gender immediately: **le menu** is masculine (*m.* or *masc.* in dictionaries) and **la valise** is feminine (*f.* or *fem.* in dictionaries).

- Does it matter? Not unless you want to make a serious attempt to speak correctly and scratch beneath the surface of the language. You would be understood if you said **la menu**, or even **le horaire**, provided your pronunciation was good.

"the" (PLURAL)

| the addresses | **les adresses** |
|---|---|
| the apples | **les pommes** |
| the bills | **les additions** |
| the cups of tea | **les tasses de thé** |
| the glasses of beer | **les verres de bière** |
| the keys | **les clés** |
| the luggage | **les bagages** |
| the menus | **les menus** |
| the newspapers | **les journaux** |
| the receipts | **les reçus** |
| the sandwiches | **les sandwichs** |
| the suitcases | **les valises** |
| the telephone directories | **les annuaires téléphoniques** |
| the schedules | **les horaires** |

- "The" is always **les** before a noun in the plural.

- Most nouns add an *s* when they are made plural, but this does not change the pronunciation: **clé** and **clés** sound the same. But watch out for many exceptions, such as **journal/journaux**.

- In French, "luggage" is always regarded as plural. It is never used to mean a single item.

Practice saying and writing the following sentences in French.

| Do you have the key? | **Avez-vous la clé?** |
|---|---|
| Do you have the luggage? | **Avez-vous…?** |
| Do you have the telephone directory? | |
| Do you have the menu? | |

| | |
|---|---|
| I would like the key. | **Je voudrais la clé.** |
| I would like the receipt. | **Je voudrais….** |
| I would like the bill. | |
| I would like the keys. | |
| Where is the key? | **Où est la clé?** |
| Where is the schedule? | **Où est…?** |
| Where is the address? | |
| Where is the suitcase? | |
| Where are the keys? | **Où sont les clés?** |
| Where are the sandwiches? | **Où sont…?** |
| Where are the apples? | |
| Where are the suitcases? | |
| Where is the luggage? | **Où sont…?** |
| Where can I get the key? | **Où puis-je trouver la clé?** |
| Where can I get the address? | **Où puis-je trouver…?** |
| Where can I get the schedules? | |

Now try to make up more sentences along the same lines. Try adding "please" (**s'il vous plaît**) at the end.

## "A"/"An" and "Some"/"Any"

| "a"/"an" (SINGULAR) | MASCULINE | FEMININE |
|---|---|---|
| an address | | **une adresse** |
| an apple | | **une pomme** |
| a bill | | **une addition** |
| a cup of tea | | **une tasse de thé** |
| a glass of beer | **un verre de bière** | |
| a key | | **une clé** |
| luggage | (*no singular*) | |
| a menu | **un menu** | |
| a newspaper | **un journal** | |
| a receipt | **un reçu** | |
| a sandwich | **un sandwich** | |
| a suitcase | | **une valise** |
| a telephone directory | **un annuaire téléphonique** | |
| a schedule | **un horaire** | |

- "A" or "an" is always **un** before a masculine noun and **une** before a feminine noun.

"some"/"any" (PLURAL)

| | |
|---|---|
| addresses | **des adresses** |
| apples | **des pommes** |
| bills | **des additions** |
| cups of tea | **des tasses de thé** |
| glasses of beer | **des verres de bière** |
| keys | **des clés** |
| luggage | **des bagages** |
| menus | **des menus** |
| journals | **des journaux** |
| receipts | **des reçus** |
| sandwiches | **des sandwichs** |
| suitcases | **des valises** |
| telephone directories | **des annuaires téléphoniques** |
| schedules | **des horaires** |

- "Some" or "any" is always **des** before a noun in the plural. In certain expressions in French, **des** is omitted. Examples of this are marked by an asterisk (*) before some of the sentences below.

Practice saying and writing these sentences in French.

| | |
|---|---|
| Do you have a receipt? | **Avez-vous...?** |
| Do you have a menu? | |
| I would like a telephone directory. | **Je voudrais....** |
| I would like some sandwiches. | |
| Where can I get some newspapers? | **Où puis-je trouver...?** |
| Where can I get a cup of tea? | |
| Is there a key? | **Est-ce qu'il y a une clé?** |
| Is there a schedule? | **Est-ce qu'il y a...?** |
| Is there a telephone directory? | |
| Is there a menu? | |
| Are there any keys? | **Est-ce qu'il y a des clés?** |
| Are there any newspapers? | **Est-ce qu'il y a...?** |
| Are there any sandwiches? | |

Now make up your own sentences along the same lines.

Try the following new phrases.

| | |
|---|---|
| I'll have .... | **Je vais prendre....** |
| I need .... | **J'ai besoin de....** |
| I'll have a glass of beer. | **Je vais prendre un verre de bière.** |

| | |
|---|---|
| I'll have a cup of tea. | **Je vais prendre….** |
| I'll have some sandwiches. | |
| I'll have some apples. | |
| I need a cup of tea. | **J'ai besoin d'une tasse de thé.** |
| I need a key. | **J'ai besoin d'….** |
| *I need some newspapers. | **J'ai besoin de journaux.** |
| *I need some keys. | **J'ai besoin de….** |
| *I need some addresses. | **J'ai besoin d'….** |
| *I need some sandwiches. | |
| *I need some suitcases. | |

In cases where "some" or "any" refers to more than one thing, such as *some/any ice cream* and *some/any tomatoes,* the word **des** is used as explained above.

| | |
|---|---|
| some/any ice cream | **des glaces** |
| some/any tomatoes | **des tomates** |

As a guide, you can usually *count* the number of containers or whole items.

In cases where "some" refers to part of a whole thing or an indefinite quantity, the word **des** cannot be used.

| | | | |
|---|---|---|---|
| the bread | **le pain** | some bread | **du pain** |
| the ice cream | **la glace** | some ice cream | **de la glace** |
| the pineapple | **l'ananas** (*masc.*) | some pineapple | **de l'ananas** |
| the tomato | **la tomate** | some tomato | **de la tomate** |
| the water | **l'eau** (*fem.*) | some water | **de l'eau** |
| the wine | **le vin** | some wine | **du vin** |

- **Du** is used for masculine nouns.

- **De la** is used for feminine nouns.

- **De l'** is used for both masculine and feminine nouns that begin with a vowel.

The same would apply to the following words. Can you complete the list below?

| | | | |
|---|---|---|---|
| the aspirin | **l'aspirine** (*fem.*) | some aspirin | _____ |
| the beer | **la bière** | some beer | _____ |
| the cheese | **le fromage** | some cheese | _____ |
| the coffee | **le café** | some coffee | _____ |
| the lemonade | **la limonade** | some lemonade | _____ |
| the tea | **le thé** | some tea | _____ |

Practice writing and saying the following sentences in French.

| | |
|---|---|
| Do you have any coffee? | **Avez-vous du café?** |
| Do you have any ice cream? | |
| Do you have any pineapple? | |
| I would like some aspirin. | **Je voudrais de l'aspirine.** |
| I would like some tomato. | |
| I would like some bread. | |
| Is there any lemonade? | **Est-ce qu'il y a de la limonade?** |
| Is there any water? | |
| Is there any wine? | |
| Where can I get some cheese? | **Où puis-je trouver du fromage?** |
| Where can I get some ice cream? | |
| Where can I get some water? | |
| I'll have some beer. | **Je vais prendre de la bière.** |
| I'll have some tea. | |
| I'll have some coffee. | |

## "This" and "That"

French uses one word to mean both "this" and "that": **ça**. If you do not know the French name for something, just point to the object and say the following.

| | |
|---|---|
| I would like that. | **Je voudrais ça.** |
| I'll have that. | **Je vais prendre ça.** |
| I need this. | **J'ai besoin de ça**. |

## Helping Others

You can help yourself by using sentences such as the following.

| | |
|---|---|
| I would like a sandwich. | **Je voudrais un sandwich.** |
| Where can I get a cup of tea? | **Où puis-je trouver une tasse de thé?** |
| I'll have a glass of beer. | **Je vais prendre un verre de bière.** |
| I need a receipt. | **J'ai besoin d'un reçu.** |

If you encounter a speaker of English who is having trouble making himself or herself understood, you should be able to speak French on the person's behalf.

| | |
|---|---|
| He would like .... | **Il voudrait un sandwich.** |
| | il voo·dreh an sahnd·wich |
| She would like .... | **Elle voudrait un sandwich.** |
| | el voo·dreh an sahnd·wich |
| Where can he get ...? | **Où peut-il trouver une tasse de thé?** |
| | oo per·teel troo·veh oon tahss der teh |
| Where can she get ...? | **Où peut-elle trouver une tasse de thé?** |
| | oo per·tel troo·veh oon tahss der teh |
| He'll have .... | **Il va prendre un verre de bière.** |
| | il vah prahnd an vair der bee·air |
| She'll have .... | **Elle va prendre un verre de bière.** |
| | el vah prahnd an vair der bee·air |
| He needs .... | **Il a besoin d'un reçu.** |
| | il ah ber·zwan dan rer·soo |
| She needs .... | **Elle a besoin d'un reçu.** |
| | el ah ber·zwan dan rer·soo |

You can also help two or more people if they are having difficulties. The two French words for "they" are **ils** (male) and **elles** (female), with **ils** also used for a group that includes both males and females. If they are a married couple, for example, the word is **ils**.

| | |
|---|---|
| They would like .... | **Ils voudraient du fromage.** |
| | il voo·dreh doo froh·mahsh |
| | **Elles voudraient du fromage.** |
| | el voo·dreh doo froh·mahsh |
| Where can they get ...? | **Où peuvent-ils trouver de l'aspirine?** |
| | oo perv·teel troo·veh der lah·speer·een |
| | **Où peuvent-elles trouver de l'aspirine?** |
| | oo perv·tel troo·veh der lah·speer·een |
| They'll have .... | **Ils vont prendre du vin.** |
| | il vohn prahnd doo van |

**Elles vont prendre du vin.**
el vohn prahnd doo van

They need ....
**Ils ont besoin d'eau.**
il·zohn ber·zwan doh

**Elles ont besoin d'eau.**
el·zohn ber·zwan doh

What about the two of you? No problem. The word for "we" is **nous**.

We would like ....
**Nous voudrions du vin.**
noo voo·dree·ohn doo van

Where can we get ...?
**Où pouvons-nous trouver de l'eau?**
oo poo·vohn·noo troo·veh der loh

We'll have ....
**Nous allons prendre de la bière.**
noo·zah·lohn prahnd der lah bee·air

We need ....
**Nous avons besoin d'aspirine.**
noo·zah·vohn ber·zwan
dah·speer·een

Try writing out your own checklist for these four useful sentence-starters, like the following.

**Je voudrais....**            **Nous voudrions....**
**Il voudrait....**            **Ils voudraient....**
**Elle voudrait....**            **Elles voudraient....**

**Où puis-je trouver...?**      **Où pouvons-nous trouver...?**
**Où peut-il trouver...?**      **Où peuvent-ils trouver...?**
**Où peut-elle trouver...?**    **Où peuvent-elles trouver...?**

## More Practice

Here are some more French names of things. Using the information given above, see how many different sentences you can make up.

|  | SINGULAR | PLURAL |
|---|---|---|
| ashtray | **cendrier** (*masc.*) | **cendriers** |
| bag | **sac** (*masc.*) | **sacs** |
| broom | **balai** (*masc.*) | **balais** |
| car | **voiture** (*fem.*) | **voitures** |
| cigarette | **cigarette** (*fem.*) | **cigarettes** |
| corkscrew | **tire-bouchon** (*masc.*) | **tire-bouchons** |
| glove | **gant** (*masc.*) | **gants** |
| ice cream | **glace** (*fem.*) | **glaces** |
| melon | **melon** (*masc.*) | **melons** |

| | SINGULAR | PLURAL |
|---|---|---|
| passport | **passeport** (*masc.*) | **passeports** |
| dish cloth | **torchon** (*masc.*) | **torchons** |
| salad | **salade** (*fem.*) | **salades** |
| saucepan | **casserole** (*fem.*) | **casseroles** |
| shoe | **chaussure** (*fem.*) | **chaussures** |
| stamp | **timbre** (*masc.*) | **timbres** |
| station | **gare** (*fem.*) | **gares** |
| street | **rue** (*fem.*) | **rues** |
| sunglasses | (*no singular*) | **lunettes de soleil** (*fem.*) |
| telephone | **téléphone** (*masc.*) | **téléphones** |
| ticket | **billet** (*masc.*) | **billets** |

# Index

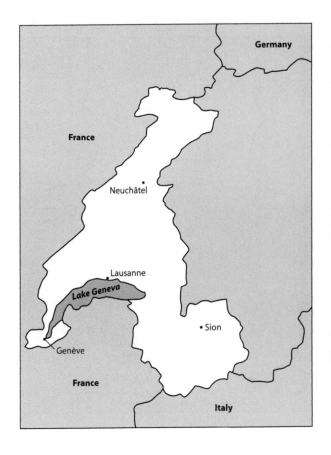